Communication Technologies And Information Flow

Pergamon Titles of Related Interest

Related Journals*

*Free specimen copies available upon request.

PERGAMON POLICY STUDIES
ON SCIENCE AND TECHNOLOGY

Communication Technologies And Information Flow

Edited by
Maxwell Lehman
Thomas J.M. Burke

Pergamon Press
NEW YORK • OXFORD • TORONTO • SYDNEY • PARIS • FRANKFURT

Pergamon Press Offices:

U.S.A.   Pergamon Press Inc., Maxwell House, Fairview Park,
                     Elmsford, New York 10523, U.S.A.

U.K.   Pergamon Press Ltd., Headington Hill Hall,
                     Oxford OX3 0BW, England

CANADA   Pergamon Press Canada Ltd., Suite 104, 150 Consumers Road,
                     Willowdale, Ontario M2J 1P9, Canada

AUSTRALIA   Pergamon Press (Aust.) Pty. Ltd., P.O. Box 544,
                     Potts Point, NSW 2011, Australia

FRANCE   Pergamon Press SARL, 24 rue des Ecoles,
                     75240 Paris, Cedex 05, France

FEDERAL REPUBLIC Pergamon Press GmbH, Hammerweg 6, Postfach 1305,
OF GERMANY   6242 Kronberg/Taunus, Federal Republic of Germany

Library of Congress Cataloging in Publication Data
Main entry under title:

Communication technologies and information flow.

   (Pergamon policy studies on science and technol-
ogy)
   Includes index.
   1. Telecommunication.   I. Lehman, Maxwell.
II. Series.
TK5101.C659 1981   621.38   80-24875
ISBN 0-08-027169-3
ISBN 0-08-027528-1 (pbk.)

Printed in the United States of America

Contents

Acknowledgments

In devising the three Communication Technology Conferences at Fairfield University from which this volume grew, the following individuals were of special help:

- Dr. Lee L. Davenport, consultant in telecommunication planning, formerly Vice-President and Chief Scientist, GTE.
- Dr. Lewis M. Branscomb, Vice-President and Chief Scientist, IBM.
- Dr. Jacob Goldman, Group Vice-President and Chief Scientist, Corporate Research and Development, Xerox Corp.
- Dr. Thomas A. Vanderslice, formerly Senior Vice-President and Sector Executive for Power Systems, GE, and now President and Chief Operating Officer, GTE.
- Robert H. Jones, Manager Power Systems Marketing and Communications Support, GE.
- Dr. Lynn W. Ellis, formerly Director of Research, IT&T, and now Vice-President Engineering, Bristol-Babcock.
- George Atherton Buckout, Department Chief Community Relations, Western Electric Co., and a member of the Advisory Committee of the Fairfield University Graduate School of Communication.

Also members of the Graduate School/Corporate Headquarters Liaison Committee, especially Dr. Joseph M. Cahalan, Manager Employee Affairs, Xerox Corp. and Adjunct Professor, Graduate School of Communication; Thomas E. McCarthy, Vice-President Public Affairs, GTE; E. James Clark, Manager Educational Programs, GE; and William J. Kenney, Director Recruiting and Executive Director of Retired Executives Programs, Economic Development Council, New York City (on loan from IBM).

- Evans Kerrigan, a 1980 graduate of The Graduate School of Communication, Fairfield University, and Arts Graphics Supervisor of Garden Way, Inc., re-did the illustrations of the articles by Dr. Richard Hayes, Raymond W. Marshall, and Dr. Lynn W. Ellis to fit the publisher's requirements.

The editors extend thanks to the <u>Smithsonian</u> and to Dr. Richard M. Restak for permission to use his article "Smart Machines Learn to See, Talk, Listen, Even 'Think' for Us."

The editors are also grateful to Bell Laboratories for permission to use the chapter by Dr. John S. Mayo entitled "VLSI: Implications for Science and Technology," copyright 1979 by Bell Telephone Laboratories, Inc. Republished with permission.

Introduction

In the late 1830s, Charles Havas of Paris began using homing pigeons to carry news between the capitals of Europe. This former banker and newspaperman, who started the Agence Havas, forerunner of the Agence France-Presse, found that he could beat the opposition in supplying international news by using these pigeons, who could fly from Paris to London in seven hours, or from Paris to Brussels in four hours. As of April 1979, Agence France-Presse, using satellites, cable, and teletype, was supplying news to newspapers, radio, and television in 154 countries, and filing 600,000 words a day. And this agency, though the oldest, is only one of five major world news agencies. The others are AP, UPI, Reuters, and Tass.

Today we can be eyewitnesses of events happening anywhere on earth or in space; a telephone call secures information virtually in any area of human knowledge, stored in international data banks; data flows continually from coast to coast and continent to continent, in a flood so vast that no one has yet determined what limits, what parameters there may be; the likelihood is there are none. And the new devices for gathering, storing, transmitting – and even initiating – information present the human mind with exhilarating possibilities. It is hardly to be wondered that some, including even scientists working in the field of communication, stand in awe of what is happening, and refer to the results of the new technology as having implications equaling those that followed the invention of printing or the industrial revolution.

In contrast to Havas' carrier pigeons, it is now possible to transmit 10,000 lines of information per minute to almost any part of the world. Any telephone in an American home or office can reach over 90 percent of all the telephones in the world. At the end of June 1980, CompuServe Inc. and Associated Press, in conjunction with other newspaper organizations, announced a joint venture to launch a nationwide electronic news delivery service which will allow anyone with a computer terminal to receive on his video screen 300 words of information a minute from the newspaper of his choice.

Since the beginning of commercial television in the early 50s, Americans have purchased (according to Don Veraksa in Advertising Age, June 2, 1980) more than 300,000,000 TV sets. Nearly half of them are still in use, and there are more of them than telephones, refrigerators, or bathtubs; at the same time, the number of radios in the country stands at a significant multiple of the population, with 48,000,000 new ones being bought in the single year of 1978. That radio, that telephone, that TV set will play increasingly interesting – indeed, vital – roles in the everyday lives of people everywhere. In addition, the slow-blooming video-disc player (a phonograph look-alike) and the video-cassette recorder (a visual equivalent of the tape recorder) are entering the market in a large way, as the minicomputer already has.

Interactive television, ranging from simple viewer response and the monitoring of fire, burglar, or medical alarms up to data bank access and, more recently, text and graphics access, is already available to some segments of the population in Europe and North America on a test basis. The same is true of direct home, office, or village reception of satellite transmissions. It is technically – although not yet commercially – possible to receive the morning newspaper right out of the television set. Video games, as any household with children can testify, have zoomed in popularity, while French card players compete by satellite with other players of belote who are seated at their tables in West Germany and Canada. Video education is already here, and will soon enter the learning arena in dramatic ways.

Microprocessors, essentially small computers inscribed on very tiny "chips" of semiconductor material, are in wide use now to provide programmed "intelligence" about many consumer products, from recorders to automobiles, from household appliances to home controls. Some experts predict that the number of microprocessors will so increase in this decade that they will surpass the "number of fingers" in the U.S. By the following decade it is expected that the new technology will bring forth devices capable not only of responding to voice signals, but answering questions. Indeed, the beginnings of such devices are already in the initial laboratory stages. Hand-held calculators, whose price started at $800 just ten years ago, cost less than $10 at the end of the decade. A new instrument using a display screen for the letters is controlled not by fingers, but by the eye movements of the typist.

What shape will the expansion of communication technologies and the explosion of innovative products give to our offices, workplaces, schools, homes, libraries, politics, business, personal lives, and society?

These technologies, and the products they produce, shape our leisure, our work, our study. They are a distinguishing mark of our current society, and they will mold our future in ways even the wisest of us cannot clearly envision.

II

Specialists in any field tend to develop an ever more extensive private vocabulary to convey a growing accumulation of sophisticated knowledge. This is not the same as the sometimes injudicious development of abstract jargon – very common to bureaucracies – which serves to obscure meaning and thus to confuse human decisions.

Lack of intelligence does not keep the average person from understanding communication technologies. Faulty scientific training may be a block, but a major obstacle is failure to understand the technology's vocabulary.

The goal of this volume is to present the latest findings of communication technologies, and to do so in language that the non-scientifically-trained reader, as well as the specialist and the student, can understand.

In this volume, a distinguished group of scientists describe the current state and the possibilities of communication technology. They present the basics of the new technologies, the quantity, accuracy, and dispersed information flow which these technologies facilitate, and the efficiencies which this flow of voice, image, and character information can bring to the home, the study, the library, the office, the school, to the large corporate organization, and to governments – not in some distant future, but today.

III

The scientists made these presentations, originally, at three conferences sponsored by the Graduate School of Corporate and Political Communication, Fairfield University, in Fairfield, Connecticut. Co-sponsors of the conferences were the headquarters of General Electric, IBM, GTE, Xerox, and the Bell System; AT&T, Western Electric, SNETCO. The active corporate cooperators were primarily the chief scientists in these firms and their associate scientists.

Since print requires a different mode than does oral presentation, the seminar participants have revised their texts for this volume.

To make it easier for the reader to position and interrelate the presentations, the following simple communications model is offered, as it was for the conference participants. It displays the basic steps followed whether one is producing the evening news, controlling one's home environment, researching an abstruse historical topic, marshalling the flow of manufacturing components, or making complex governmental or corporate decisions. The communication technologies presented, no matter how dazzling their contemporary results or how awesome their implications for society, are rooted in the basic functions here illustrated. Around these functions cluster the innovative systems and products.

Dr. Lee L. Davenport, who greatly helped shape the conferences, presents an overview. Communication, he says, distinguishes the human social system from animal social systems.

In our time, the development of input devices from the transistor to integrated circuits, and from integrated circuits to solid state memories, microprocessors, optics, and lasers, has given to the human communication of information the characteristics of an "electronic information age." And, he adds, "we are only at the beginning."

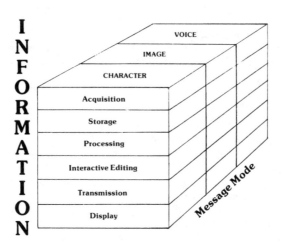

Fig. I.1. A communication process model.

Dr. P.E. Pashler gives historical perspective to the development of technologies for storing print, images, and sound. From the earliest information storage technology, writing on clay tablets, society eventually developed printing, which changed education, affected the industrial revolution, the character of democratic society, and man's mode of perception. Dr. Pashler makes a distinction between storage technologies whose output has direct impact on the human senses, and those whose input and output is only in relation to machines.

In our time, storage technologies have been developed for images, sound, and characters, from photographs to film and video, from records to tapes. Dr. Pashler describes the latest of these technologies – machines that both write and read while humans may never be involved in the actual content that is read or written. He describes some of the latest memory developments utilizing magnetic bubbles, where no mechanical motion is involved; and he explores the possibilities of archival memories, which can store and retrieve staggering amounts of data, and could make it possible to secure specific information on request from the millions of volumes and tens of millions of items held by massive facilities like the Library of Congress.

Dr. Pashler ends with the optimistic assertion that "whenever we have a major breakthrough in information storage technology, we obtain a tremendous release of the creative powers of humanity."

Dr. Lynn W. Ellis notes that of all the activities listed in the communication process model, only the transmission function is international in scope. "While the information content of the other functions may be intended for international audiences, the generation activity takes place within national boundaries. It is the transmission function which crosses these boundaries, bringing with it opportunities and problems." He discusses international telecommunication technologies which facilitate character, image, and voice transmission. The economics and efficiencies of submarine cables versus satellites are discussed, as well as some of the current controversy about transborder data-flows.

B. H. Burdine begins his description of satellite communication transmission with Arthur C. Clark's 1945 proposal that geosynchronous (that is, effectively stationary) satellites powered by solar energy could provide worldwide communications. From the launch in the mid-1960s of the first commercial communication satellite, there has been a progression toward ever larger satellites and ever smaller earth stations. Mr. Burdine details some of the difficulties caused by sun, rain, and crowding. He concludes with the description of a super-satellite which could allow 25,000,000 users to communicate by wrist telephones, or could be used for electronic mail connecting 500,000 offices, each with a roof-top antenna. It could also provide educational TV for 80,000 schools or video-conferencing from 500 studios.

There has been much discussion of automated factories and automated processes, but only now is attention focusing on the office.

Utilizing the office as an illustrative focus, Dr. R.J. Hayes describes the role of the image – meaning graphics and graphic technology – in the generation, processing, communicating, storing, and reproducing of information. He predicts that a much larger capital investment per worker in the office environments, for technology, will improve productivity.

The criteria he uses in evaluating graphic technology developments are: improving productivity, improving response time, improving performance, and containing costs. The target for the development and adoption of the technology is to enhance the flow of information, which includes generation and revision, printing and reproduction, distribution and communication, filing and retrieval.

Most developments in graphics he sees as being evolutionary. Soft display will remain important in new applications. But, he notes, technologists are continuing to work on systems like laser xerography and ink jet to improve reliability, and to lower cost and noise. This could result in revolutionary changes in non-impact printing, hard copy graphics, and the development of compact, noiseless devices.

Dr. E. Bryan Carne considers future household communication-information systems. All of the technology now exists for this "future" communications home.

Today, the household depends on radio, television, and telephone for entertainment, information, social contacts, and assistance. These communication media have changed the way we live.

But burgeoning technology, as Carne observes, makes possible other media and services which may further affect our lifestyles. "Concepts exist for revolutionary household communication-information systems, and limited trials have been made."

In his paper, he speculates on some of the needs which may shape future systems. He notes current demonstrations and trials of advanced communication-information systems around the world, describes three specialized terminals now being tested in the laboratory, and reviews anticipated technical progress which may facilitate future developments.

Finally, he proposes the concept of a total home communication system. But, he suggests, some existing market forces may restrict the development of a fully unified system.

J. Raymond Marshall presents the combination of available technology and demands of business which make worldwide information service possible, desired, and necessary. Much of today's literature dwells on how small devices are becoming: we read about mini-computers, microcomputers, microprocessors and, in the area of communications, we discuss fiber optics and laser beam technology. But, as Marshall explains, the evolution at the upper end of computing and communications is just as dramatic. We now have more powerful computational capacity than ever before in a single entity, and we can communicate at higher speeds and over longer distances than ever before. The intersection of computing and communications comprises the new world of informational services.

Using the General Electric Information Services Company's MARK III Service as the basis for most of his discussion, Marshall explains some of the techniques used in the areas of generation, transmission, and distribution to bring service quality up to the 99½ to 100 percent level. To achieve this necessitated using special "clustering" techniques to overcome the inherent lack of such near-perfect quality in the manufactured computer; it also required technological innovations to nullify short-term or long-term outages (failure) of communication. He describes the "store and forward" techniques employed, and the reasons for simultaneous use of satellite circuits and undersea cable.

He uses four examples to illustrate how worldwide information service interrelates with business enterprise.

Dr. Joseph Agresta describes in detail the current technologies and how and why they will change the office in the next five to ten years.

He does not try to foretell the exact nature of that office, but he discounts the vision, on the one hand, of a dehumanized "1984" society controlled by machines and a small elite of technocrats, and the vision, on the other hand, of a leisure-oriented utopia where everyone works out of his or her own home and deals with the world through a myriad of wondrous electronic devices.

The path to the office of the future, in his view, is evolutionary. After discussing the various technologies, their potentials, and implications, he presents the phased scenario which he believes makes the most sense for most organizations. In stage I, word processors are used for typing and editing, and initial efforts at electronic filing and retrieval are made. In stage II, the rudiments of electronic mail develop, and access to computers is used for data to be incorporated into reports. In stage III, electronic mail/message systems play a large role, while administrative work stations for non-word processing applications develop, and administrative support systems for travel, scheduling, etc. are implemented. In stage IV, management work stations enable the manager to deal directly with all the systems.

James M. West offers some refreshing caveats concerning our love affair with the office of the future. He describes some of the barriers that keep the people involved from enthusiastically welcoming changes in their work place. These range from the possibility that mechanized systems will be oversold as surrogates of truly automated systems, to installing new systems which appear to threaten personal control or cause physical fatigue and eye irritation. He sees the fear of losing control as a major issue in resistance to change. If a new system does not duplicate present controls or provide equivalent controls, there are problems for everyone, from the executive to the clerical workers to those who perform routine tasks. Also, West states, if a new system forces people to operate in entirely different ways, both managers and secretaries will use only some of its features and never fully adopt it.

He considers the multifunction work station to be the real beginning of the office of the future. Driven by a mini- or macrocomputer, it has gateways to various communication networks, it has document-creation ability to capture key strokes and graphics, and it can display or create hard copy or send a message.

Substantial steps to the office of the future will be taken when the technology of communication systems links with the science of systems management and, when necessary, with the behavioral sciences, to produce arrangements that highlight critical and significant information, whether process or communication oriented, for the decision maker to act upon.

Jean Raymond Marchand provides a case history, dealing with two demonstration projects, one in a rural setting and the other beamed across Canada.

The first is a field trial of fiber optics in a tiny town, population 300, in Manitoba. Some 27 percent of Canadians live in rural areas.

There is a tremendous gap between rural and urban communication, because the cost of rural transmission is so steep. The optimism behind this demonstration is based on the fact that communications technology can be so accelerated as to lead to lower prices.

Using a single fiber (a spare fiber will also be installed) from a distribution center to the home, the following services will be provided: single party telephones for every subscriber (multi-party phones are not uncommon); eight or nine video channels; seven FM radio channels; and a basic data-receiving capability. The spare fiber could be used to try video-interactive communications.

The second demonstration, utilizing a satellite to cover most of Canada, emphasizes tele-medicine and tele-education, and in addition carries communications originated and produced by native people, Indian and Eskimo. The ability of rural areas, even isolated ones, to generate and receive information on a basis virtually equal to such capabilities in urban centers, will have a profound impact on governmental, political, economic and educational aspects of society. The availability of information has historically evoked enormous societal changes. It is fair speculation that we are arriving at another such landmark in human development.

Dr. Richard M. Restak describes some of the newest computer-assisted devices that can talk, listen, answer questions, explain answers, and respond to commands as subtle as a change in one's eye position.

Motor-injured persons, for instance, can now type by merely looking at the letters on a display unit. The device responds to the position of the eye. No finger or hand movements are necessary. After several hours of practice, volunteers have achieved a speed of 18 words a minute – and with few errors – about half the speed of a public relations person typing with two fingers.

Dr. Restak describes other areas now being explored, among them being the development of machines with pattern recognition, inference, and "intelligence" capabilities; and some of their applications in medicine, language training, and cooperative ventures with humans in manipulating hostile environments.

In the area of games, Dr. Restak surmises that an inexpensive programmed computer will soon be able to beat all but the best chess players in the world. But, at this writing, superior players can still outplay even a massive computer, because instead of trying out large numbers of potential moves as a computer would, they ponder only a relatively small number of promising moves, highly intuitive, original, and idiosyncratic. These human characteristics cannot yet be duplicated by computers.

Dr. John S. Mayo describes the progress and application of the technology utilized in Very Large Scale Integrated (VLSI) circuits. These circuits promise accomplishments that will likely dwarf today's electronic revolution.

Since the integrated circuit industry began in 1960, the number of components per chip of silicon has constantly increased. Today over 150,000 components can be fabricated and interconnected on a single chip about one-tenth the size of a postage stamp. Dr. Mayo estimates that it is technologically feasible to have more than one billion components per chip.

VLSI offers low-cost electronics, remarkable reliability, small size, and energy saving. It is a technology of the microscopic world. It has stimulated a wide range of developments for dealing with physical features of micron dimensions. It will increasingly affect business, education, data processing, and communications.

The industrial revolution, by harnessing mechanical energy to augment the muscles, greatly changed the world. The electronics revolution, by harnessing the electron to augment the mind of man, has, in a little over thirty years, effected great changes in the United States and has touched every part of the world.

Dr. Mayo calls data processing and telecommunications extensions of the mind: "They speed up mental processes by greatly reducing the time required for doing analysis and for interacting with both minds and machines."

VLSI deeply affects both telecommunications and data processing. As VLSI progresses, Mayo predicts that it will produce startling new developments with profound implications for the future. "It is a rich source of ideas and tools for a wide range of industries. Ultimately it is up to society as a whole to determine how it uses the ideas and tools supplied by technology and this holds true for VLSI."

Thomas J.M. Burke
Maxwell Lehman

1 Technology and the Communication Society: An Informal Overview

Lee L. Davenport

A new era in the communication of information is upon us. Communications technology is exploding and is rapidly being put to use. It is relevant to ask: Where is this taking us? Why do we speak of a "communication society"?

Let me start this overview by clarifying what I mean by a "communication society." A primary element of the human social system is what we call <u>communication</u>. Communication is a basic feature distinguishing the <u>human social</u> system. What we communicate is information, and what concerns us here is information – the form in which it appears and how that form is changing.

Some people have called what is happening the "information revolution." They refer to it as a revolution in order to draw a parallel with the industrial revolution and dignify this new change by investing it with an importance equalling that of the industrial revolution.

THE PAPER INFORMATION AGE

We live today in a paper information age. In every area of business and commerce, government, law, education, and health, our transactions are mainly paper documents. We have letters, memoranda, reports, specifications, executive orders, written policies, documentation, notes – we're swamped with paper. Your desk and mine show the state of the paper information age. Sometimes there's hardly room for a coffee cup in the office. The stuff overflows on credenzas and chairs, even in the classiest executive offices.

When we go to a meeting, we must be prepared. We bring our files, our reports. Somehow this has to be our refresher for our mental storage system, so we carry our material along. To support all this, there are the secretaries.

We also must have, close at hand, information stored in files, so outside every office stand the filing cabinets. Heaven help us if the

1

secretary isn't there to find what's in the filing cabinets. These local files are backed up by central files, row on row on row. Handling paper-stored information is a slow, complex job. It's made easier, or more complex perhaps, depending on how you want to view it, by our friends from Xerox, who help us to have at least five copies of everything – usually more copies to fill more files – but at least somebody can find the copy when you need it.

Now, how do we communicate with each other in the midst of this paper revolution?

One means is by mail, the carrier of our paper transactions since ancient times. We've entrusted our commercial and social lifelines to the post office. Over the pillars on the front of a New York Post Office building is chiseled this motto: "Neither rain nor snow nor gloom of night shall stay these couriers from the swift completion of their appointed rounds." The motto says nothing about growling dogs or strikes, but it does imply that the postal service (which although lately much maligned, has served this nation relatively well) continues to carry most of our communications.

The postal service's information system is slow, occupies lots of space, and is increasing in cost. Today it costs A¢ to mail a letter. Next week or next year it may cost B¢, but it will surely be higher than B¢ sometime after that. There must be a better way. There _is_ a better way, of course. That's what the information revolution is all about.

ELECTRONIC INFORMATION

The new technologies enable us to take transaction documents and store the information in them economically by electronic means.

Not only can we store information electronically, quickly; we can process it electronically, transmit it electronically, and retrieve it when we want it – all at incredibly high speeds. This information is in the form of electrical impulses, or bits, or digits. Computers operate by pulses and perform electronic storage. The telephone network also uses pulses, and transmits electronic signals to provide instant tele-communications. This instant telecommunication is becoming available everywhere.

Take one example, an office, specifically a stockbroker's office: Many brokers' offices contain a terminal, an input-output device. This terminal is the basic form of all of our first-generation electronic information terminals. It has a cathode ray tube or some other display, a keyboard, and a wire which connects it to the outside world. For stockbrokers, the keyboard is alphabetically oriented, so all the user has to do is push a single key to request various kinds of useful stock data.

The awareness of services like instant stock quotations systems is reaching the general business world, and costs are coming down rapidly. In fact, even the hobbyist can now build his or her own information terminal for the home, or even have a home computer. In every case, there's a cathode ray tube display and a keyboard – and no paper.

This new era is not a dream. It's here. The uses of electronic data systems are becoming widely prevalent. Paper systems keep going up in price; electronic storage systems keep coming down in price.

The main present replacement for the transmission of paper information by mail is some form of wire network. It is largely the telephone network, although there is evidence that satellite communications or the cable TV networks will play a role in the future. Electronic mail and electronic newspapers are foreseeable realities.

Solid State Devices, Laser, Optics

There has to be behind the scenes some new technology that has made it all possible – and indeed there is. That technology is based upon what are known as solid state devices, essentially the 1948 invention called the transistor. Out of the transistor has come integrated circuits, and integrated circuits have produced solid-state memories, micro-processors, and a variety of other devices.

Parallel with that has been the development of a new technology in optics based upon the laser and optical fibers, which can make use of laser signals. The lasers and the optical fibers also operate ideally with digital information.

Before we go further, let me answer in advance one question that should come to mind. Although there has been much progress, what will happen in the near future? Are we running dry? I can answer that for you with a firm "No"! We are not running dry. The technology is moving swiftly, and we can predict advances at least as far ahead as 1990. Beyond that, our vision becomes dimmer.

Transistors

The whole thing started with the invention of the transistor at Bell Labs. The transistor is a device that was conceived as a replacement for the vacuum tube. Integrated circuits grew out of the transistor and are the foundation for the most important development in the history of electronics. These tiny circuits have made the modern computer possible, and are appearing in all sorts of devices and systems.

When they first appeared, transistors cost about a dollar each. They were widely used in small pocket radios that cost about $35.00. You can go to the drugstore today and pick up one for $4.95. Inside today's version are little transistors in cans much smaller than aspirin tablets. Today's most modern integrated circuits can hold 64,000 bits of information. The ones coming off the production line today are about 16 kilobit memories, and 64 kilobit versions are beginning to appear.

OPTICAL CHARACTER RECOGNITION

All the input devices we need to feed this electronic information age are here today. Solid state cameras are here at reasonable cost to help feed the information systems. Complete electronic keyboards are available at reasonable cost. Probably one of the most difficult-to-make input devices for changing information into electronic form is one that will read printed material. Optical Character Recognition (OCR) is a field that has had significant research applied to it. OCR devices have been around for quite a while and have had many problems.

The first ones that I can remember cost $500,000 and would read only one particular style of typewritten typeface. Today they are becoming simpler, less costly, and are required for translating the paper information age into the electronic information age. Optical character recognition is moving rapidly. We are at a point where we can automatically read printed information, and translate that information into electronic digital form which we can then manipulate in a variety of ways.

I want to close by telling you about a small company in Cambridge, Massachusetts, Kurzweil Computer Products. Kurzweil has perfected an optical character reader that will read books out loud to blind people. That's a much more difficult task than making the kind of input device we need for our electronic revolution. The Kurzweil device will read almost any type size, and any font commonly used in books. It will read italics and typewritten pages. It will read a whole word, look up the pronunciation of that word in its memory, accent the word correctly, phrase a sentence, check where the period is at the end of a sentence, and conclude that sentence correctly on a down note, just as a human speaker would. Or, if there is a question mark, it will end the sentence on an up pitch. It will read at almost any speed up to 250 words a minute. The device is the size of two breadboxes.

The Kurzweil reader solves a problem that would have confounded the most complex of our computers only a decade ago. Here today is a $19,400 mechanism, based largely on microprocessors and electronic memory, that will enable blind people to read. It takes only a fraction of that device – none of the pronunciation, much less the memory – to form the optical character reader inputs that we will need for our electronic information era.

And we're only at the beginning.

2 Information Storage Technologies
P.E. Pashler

Let's consider the storage of information. I want to suggest two different paths to establish a framework for understanding the trends in information storage technology. I make a distinction between (a) those information storage technologies whose output directly impacts on the human senses, our eyes and ears, and (b) those information storage technologies which input and output only to machines. If we are to see this new technology in perspective, we have to view what is happening today as being part of a continuing historical movement.

What do we mean by information storage technology? One example is ancient writing on clay tablets. Many of these tablets are still extant, and can be read and decoded. Some tell of great feats of early civilization. Others tell how many bags of corn were produced on such and such a farm. A later example is the Dead Sea scrolls, on papyrus, one of the most fascinating findings in archaeological history. Then, monks of the Middle Ages who illuminated manuscripts preserved, with primitive but beautiful technology, the learning and culture of society at that time.

In all of these examples we are talking about the written word. Writing, whether on stone or clay or parchment or paper, embodies one of the most important inventions of humankind: the use of symbols to represent words and numbers. The invention of written word technology involved a high degree of skill. It probably was at least as rare in its time as skill in electronics technology is today.

INNOVATIONS IN COMMUNICATIONS

Movable Type

The next major information storage innovation was the movable type press of Gutenberg. This made available an immense amount of

5

material printed on paper. The characteristics of the printed word are that we again represent symbols, but now we reproduce them by machine, while a human has to read them.

There has been a history of continuing development with respect to paper and ink. Printing technology has been around for 500 years, yet even the last decade has seen major changes in that technology. And of course the range of applications is enormous.

Consider the impact on society. Let me give just a few examples of things that I think it's pretty clear would not have happened without the development of printing technology: general education, the industrial revolution, democratic society.

Images

Now, let's look at another kind of information — that represented by images predating the written or printed word. Fifteen thousand years ago, people living in caves at the edge of a polar ice cap had the urge and the skill to produce pictures, representations of reality. Or consider a more recent use of the picture image, an architectural rendering by Thomas Jefferson. It is the characteristic of such images that they can be used to represent things; no intervening symbols are needed. Considerable skill on the part of the creator of the image, but essentially little skill on the part of the viewer, is required to look at the image and interpret it. There is a universality in the picture.

A development analogous to the printing press has been the photograph. Photography is 150 years old, and its handmaiden is the moving picture. They are present everywhere and have exerted a profound influence on our lives.

Another aspect of photography is represented by electromicrographs, which can convey an image of immeasurably tiny objects. Bacteriophage, for example, is a sub-microscopic organism. The dimensions of a bacteriophage pod are about 500 angstroms, a unit of measurement based on wavelength of light. That is something like a fiftieth of the dimension of a human hair. Yet we can see the finest structure; and this is not the ultimate of what is possible with electron microscopy.

Behind the photographic process is a highly sophisticated body of technology. The cameras, the lens, the films themselves. It doesn't take very much skill to look at a photograph and get a great deal out of it; and the photographic image has had impact on almost every segment of human activity. Those were all inputs that appealed to the eye as the principal human sense.

INFORMATION STORAGE ON RECORDS AND TAPE

A century ago, Thomas Edison built a phonograph, the device that created the record — what we will refer to as the read-in, in the jargon of information storage technology, and similar to the play-back or read-out mechanism. A sound wave impinges on the horn and the energy is concentrated, a diaphragm is moved, and a needle is driven to put little scratches on a waxed disc. The play-back process is the inverse. This technology has come a long way. An immense range, from sophistication to low-cost realism, is now available to the user, a variety of recorded material that defies imagination.

Another important development in the audio storage world is, of course, the magnetic tape that came about post-World War II. Tape recording machines are available in a variety of configurations, among them reel-to-reel type and cassette.

Modern audio provides an almost unbelievably accurate reproduction of sound. Machines are involved, true, but they are primarily making an exact replica to the human senses. The technologies are sophisticated. One of the significant breakthroughs was the introduction of the long-play record. Those of you who were interested at that time will remember that there was a considerable impediment because of the incompatability between the 33 1/3 rpm record and the 45s. That now has been resolved pretty much in favor of the 33, but the conflict between the two speeds held back the production and advancement of that technology for a number of years.

In the mid-fifties we had the advent of the stereophonic sound. Later quadrophonics. Stereo was here to stay. Quadrophonic, I think, is still questionable.

The tape material world has advanced with substantial diversity and also with a variety of qualities and characteristics. This is one of the areas of differentiation and one of the areas of advance in the audio world.

The audio cassette was a useful development because it got rid of all the handling of those reel-to-reel tapes which were a barrier to their wide use. It's a trivial thing to make an audio recording. The equipment is small. You have all seen these hand recorders the size of a cigarette package (of course, the quality is not very high in these small instruments).

One of the interesting recent developments has been a system that gets rid of the background hiss that characterized much of the earlier sound recordings.

"BORROWING" INFORMATION STORAGE

A characteristic of development that we see again and again is how one information storage technology application borrows from another. A case in point is the adaption of tape recording to video, once it had been perfected for the recording of audio. Technologically it presents an intricate problem. You have to record, in terms of rate, something like one hundred to two hundred times as much information in a video tape as you do in an audio tape. The first machines here were introduced in the mid-fifties. They used a two-inch wide tape moving at considerable velocity. Next they were reduced in size, and a portable system can now be used by cameramen off-site, away from the studio for portable pickups. Inevitably, people have been miniaturizing these still further to make the instrument a consumer product.

Modern news broadcasting is to a high degree a product of the advances in this technology. The techniques, the machinery, and the medium are intrinsically costly and sophisticated. After the first use in the world of TV broadcasting, this technology spread into instructional and other uses with simpler equipment.

The potential of video tape recording was recognized almost from the beginning, and a number of companies undertook developments in this field. For various reasons, most American companies decided it was probably not going to be worthwhile as a business venture. The Japanese persisted, and achieved breakthroughs in the development of equipment that can record for two hours, even four hours, selling for under a thousand dollars and costing between ten and twenty dollar for one hour's recording.

COST PROJECTIONS FOR STORAGE TECHNOLOGIES

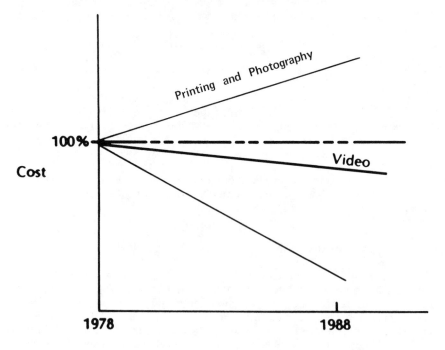

Fig. 2.1.

As often happens in technology, those kinds of developments resulted from a number of independent approaches to the problem. We have the Sony Betamax, the VHS system of Japanese Victor. Even within one company, Matsushita, which also owns Japanese Victor, there is separate development. They are all competitive, but they have the intrinsic problem that none of them are compatible. If you buy one system you can't play the recordings of another manufacturer on it. That is what I refer to as the Tower of Babel, which is certainly holding back the introduction of this technology into everyday use.

Chicken and Egg

Another aspect of this problem is what I refer to as the chicken and the egg.   What it means is that if you are, let's say, a producer of programming and you would like to make a two-hour movie using this technology, you would have considerable expense, a minimum of $1000 a minute. If you wanted to make a really tremendous spectacular, it could cost you $100,000 a minute. Would you make that kind of an investment in production alone unless you knew you could sell it?

The other side of the coin is, would you, as a potential purchaser of this kind of equipment, pay $1000 for a machine to play a movie, maybe one out of twenty to fifty titles available, most which you may have seen at your neighborhood cinema? That is the chicken and the egg problem associated with the home video system. I don't know how it is going to be resolved. It was the early recognition of this fundamental deterrent that caused American companies to say "thanks but we will pass up that one."

VIDEO DISC

A kindred development is the video recording disc. You are going to see several kinds on the market, but there are two major classes. The video disc system has been developed somewhat independently by Philips and MCA, who have subsequently decided to marry their interests. MCA is Music Corporation of America, holders of thousands of old movies as well as one of America's leading production companies. Philips is the Philips Gloelampfabrike Company of Holland. Instead of a needle in a groove, a laser beam is focussed on a point on the disc. Spiral recording tracks are held in close focus on the surface of the disc. The modulation of that laser light beam by the record produces a video signal that can be played out over your television set. The recording itself is a series of very, very fine dots. With automatic electronic mechanisms it is possible to keep that focussed on just the track you want, producing exceptionally fine pictures.

Here is a recording system that, when I first heard about it, I guess my jaw literally dropped because I would have said, like most people knowledgeable in the art, that this could not be done. You remember I said there is somewhere between one and two hundred times the amount of information involved in video recording. In any case, German engineers at Telefunken developed this in Berlin. It involves a pickup, analogous to the pickup in your present phonograph. There is a groove in a recording of the type common in a 33 1/3 phonograph record. Under the groove, occupying about the same width, are ten or more tracks of this new Teldec type of recording.

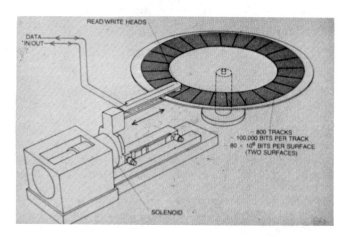

Fig. 2.2. Magnetic disc memory.

We see here, incidentally, that an essential part of the information revolution is our ability to miniaturize and to microize, rather than just reduce in size, to take something from quite large to invisibly small, and still have meaningful function and content in it.

A variant of this is the RCA video disc which, instead of using a piezo electric or crystal pickup, uses a capacitor. It is in the same family as the Teldec. The Philips and the MCA are primarily optical; the others are contact recordings. As I understand it, the Teldec system, the German system, went on the market for awhile in Germany and is now withdrawn. RCA put a substantial investment not only in the research side but in production capabilities, and that is also now "on hold." It is on hold for the reasons I mentioned earlier in connection with the tapes — the Tower of Babel and the Chicken and the Egg problems. Those are real stoppers for this business. The Japanese, however, are continually working at it, and maybe by persistence will win out in this field.

A significant difference between this type of system and tape recording is the fact that here we have a pressed vinyl record as distinct from a roll of tape. A roll of magnetic tape is intrinsically rather costly. While one can expect that still smaller and smaller areas will be required, it is not cheap now, and I can't imagine how it will ever be as cheap as a pressed vinyl recording. The cost of a vinyl recording, leaving aside all of the production or artistic costs and considering just the material machinery costs, is not more than a dollar for roughly an hour's recording.

All these systems of information storage technologies involve an "appeal" to human senses.

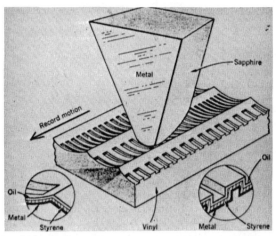

Fig. 2.3. RCA video disc.

MACHINES DO IT WITHOUT HUMANS

Now, I would like to describe the other class of technologies, where the machine both writes and reads, and humans may never be involved in the actual content that is read and written. To start, let's look at why we have to have this storage technology in connection with machines. The basic point is: when you work with a simple numbering system one, two, three, four, five and so on, you have distinct symbols for each of the digits. The binary digital system used in most present day machines requires only two numerals, zero and one. In the binary system, a one is a one, a two is a ten (10) and a five is a hundred and one (101), and so on. You see, any number can be made using only zero and one. The important thing from the viewpoint of storage technology is that central block, the storage memory.

In addition to doing simple arithmetic things, a modern computer can do a great deal more. It can read, it can encode letters, and from that we can create files. One of the earliest and the most intriguing file systems was the airline reservation system: almost anywhere in the world you can go to an airline office and instantly find out about availability of space from, say Bangor to Singapore. If you pick up a phone you can book right through (if there is airplane space). Needless to say, our friends in the Internal Revenue Service probably have a file on most of us. (Let's hope it is a pretty inactive one.) Given this machine capability, you can now search, you can retrieve, you can abstract from a file, you can even do transactions.

Operating on Sound

Another use of digital technology is operating on sound. We can sample sound intensity at a high enough frequency so that there is no possibility of the sampling process reducing intelligibility or high fidelity. It is possible to create a visual image using sound. In this case we take the image field, the flat square or rectangle of the image, and we scan along point by point as in television and we record both the light intensity in binary form, and the color of that point. So we can input or output a complete image from the machine.

The principal user and driver in storage technology is of course, the digital computer. It is common in computers to break the storage function up into a hierarchy of memory. The reason reflects one of the problems engineers face in the real world: you get one desirable characteristic at the expense of another. So you make trade-offs. The trade-offs in this hierarchical system are among the following types. First, are the very fast memories which can keep up with the fastest kind of manipulations done in the logic. They are expensive and we call them first class – the scratch pad memories. Next are the working memories of a computer, the type that do most of the regular work, and are less costly. We then have a wide range of slower memory systems.

Drums, Discs, Tapes, Bubbles

When we go to the slower memories, we are mostly in the region of mechanically accessed types. I am referring to drums, discs, and tapes. For a long time there was a gap between those sets of ellipses. Recently it has been possible to fill that gap with two types of static memories – CCD's and magnetic bubbles (with no mechanical motion).

Let me briefly explain what is involved in some of those. Most integrated circuits at this scale look pretty much alike. They are small, about a quarter of an inch square. The actual storage of information takes place at the intersection of the vertical and horizontal warp and woof. They look rather like a textile, and just from appearance, unless you are very knowledgeable, you would have a hard time looking at a chip and saying which is a scratch pad memory and which is a working memory. Technology people use terms like MOS RAM, in which MOS means metal oxide semi-conductor, and RAM means random access memory. To this is added 16,000 bits, which refers to the number of zeros and ones that can be stored on the circuit. And of course it doesn't matter what those 16,000 bits represent; they can be numbers or part of a computation, they can be letters, they can represent light intensity or colors.

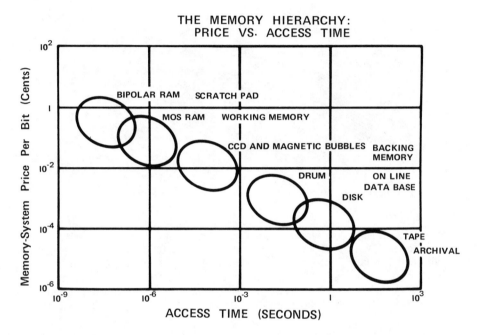

**THE MEMORY HIERARCHY:
PRICE VS. ACCESS TIME**

Fig. 2.4.

Magnetic bubbles make use of an important property of magnetic materials recently discovered and developed. With them one can create domains of magnetization which are highly mobile in a plane, in a thin film of special magnetic materials. If we apply a magnetic field to a film of material which is perpendicular to the plane of the film, and then raise that magnetic field, we turn these magnetic domains more and more to one polarity. They may almost all become north, since there is shrinkage of the south magnetizations. Finally we have little isolated domains. Now we find minute objects that we call bubbles. An important property of the magnetic bubbles is that it is highly mobile in the film. Bubbles act almost like billiard balls. They can be moved around the film like billiard balls on a table.

If you were to look at an enlarged photograph of magnetic bubbles, you would observe another property. You would see a dark line, perhaps on the lower left of the photo. That dark line is an auxiliary magnetic field, which is not in the plane but along the surface. On one side of that line there are a lot of bubbles, while on the other side there are practically none. If we were to wave a wand over those bubbles they would follow. Using these phenomena, a number of interesting memories have been derived. The way that is done is to deposit certain patterns of magnetic materials on the surface of these films. That uses technology from the world of the integrated circuit.

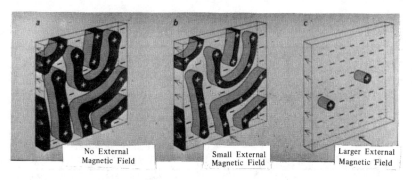

Fig. 2.5. Magnetic bubbles.

Now let's move on to the world of magnetic discs. In a typical computer room you would find a substantial number of magnetic disc memories. Discs look like phonograph records, but they are not pressed vinyl, they are magnetic material, very much like that used for magnetic tapes. We have pickup not with contact like a needle in a record groove, but with little coils of wire. We have a mechanism to move that pickup head radially in and out, while the disc itself is rotated.

The magnetic disc has an interesting kid brother called the floppy disc. This kid brother is going to be a very important component for the new information systems, like the $500 computer for use in the home. It is already possible to get a floppy disc with capacity in the neighborhood of ten million bits for about $400. And that price is undoubtedly going to come down.

We should also mention archival memory. That is coming to have a special meaning for very large on-line data storage. Archival memories are intended to store staggering quantities of data. They store data permanently, and can retrieve them relatively slowly.

There are a lot of things being examined for archival memories. Among them are magnetic tapes, video discs, and extremely tiny recordings using the electron microscope. What would we really do with this? One of the problems is how to organize it. Imagine the sheer size of an index to the Library of Congress. Any of you who have tried to get information out of a major library, a library with millions of volumes and tens of millions of items, knows what a formidable task that is. When we have a huge amount of data it might as well be lost unless we have an information system that enables us to access the information we actually want.

What is on the horizon and what is beyond it? Cost will be an important factor in what happens. Printing, photography, and paper will get more and more costly. I don't expect the world of video to experience drastic price reductions. But the cost of digital machine technology is certainly going to decrease, at least for the next decade. Digital technology will be the driver in the world of information storage.

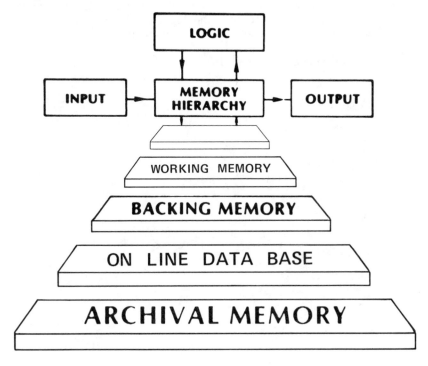

Fig. 2.6.

What is going to be possible? Here are a few things:

- We could mechanize a library.
- We could have electronic mail.
- We can have systems in our homes such as View Data, now going into use in Great Britain and in continental Europe. With these you can call up all kinds of current information, prices or travel schedules, weather or road information by simply requesting it through your telephone system, and seeing it on your TV tube.

We have to face up to quite a few problems that come with the technology. There is the problem of how to organize the systems and how to organize the information. We have the problems of the diversity of systems – will they be able to talk to each other? Another question is whether people will agree to the release of copyrights and on what terms. This library of the future is not going to be of much use if every publisher says "Go ahead but you can't have my books in it."

I am optimistic about these potentials, though, because history demonstrates that whenever we have a major breakthrough in information storage technology we obtain a tremendous release of the creative powers of humanity. I think that is the promise of the current revolution in information storage technology, and I know we are only at the beginning of the applications of this technology.

[See Appendix, pages 17 to 21.]

APPENDIX A

THE WRITTEN WORD

Characteristics

- Symbols Represent Words and Numbers
- Written Manually (Human)
- Read Visually (Human)
- Writer and Reader Were Literate (Skilled Human)
- Applications Ranged from the Mundane to the Sublime

THE PRINTED WORD

Characteristics

- Symbols Written by Machine
- Read Visually (Human)
- Needs Paper, Ink, Printing Technology
- Infinite Range of Applications
- A Necessary Condition for
  - Universal Education
  - The Industrial Revolution
  - Democratic Institutions

THE IMAGE

Characteristics

- Identifiable Images Represent Things
- Drawn Manually (Human Skill)
- Observed by the Human Eye (No Skill)
- Universal Applications

THE PHOTOGRAPH

Characteristics

- Highly Realistic Images Represent Things
- Simple to "Take" Pictures
- Backup of Sophisticated Technologies in Cameras, Film
- Observed by Human Eye (No Skill)
- Universal Applications

AUDIO

Characteristics

- Provides Accurate Sound Recording
- Uses Machines for Recording (Writing) and Reading (Playback)
- Needs Sophisticated Technologies for Records, Tapes
- Simple To Use, Especially for Playback

AUDIO TECHNOLOGY ADVANCES

Discs

- Long Play Records (Late 40's)
- 33 1/3 RPM vs. 45 RPM
- Stereo (Mid 50's)
- 4 Channel Sound (Late 60's)

Tapes

- Improved Tape Materials
- Audio Cassettes
- Miniaturized Equipment
- Noise Reduction Techniques

VIDEO

Tape Recording

- Introduced in TV Studios (Late 50's)
- Major Changes in Programming and Production Techniques
- Intrinsically Costly and Sophisticated Medium and Equipment
- Closed Circuit (Instructional, Etc.) Use Begun in Mid 60's
- Home Entertainment Potential Recognized Early by Many Contenders
- U.S. Companies Drop Out
- Japanese Introduce 2- and 4-Hour Recordings; Costs Under $1,000
- Medium Costs are $10 to $20 Per Hour
- 4 Competing Systems

SYSTEM	SPONSOR	TIME	PRICE
Beta	Sony	2 Hours	$900-$1,050
VHS	Japanese Victor	4 Hours	$850-$1,050
VX	Matsushita	2 Hours	$895
V-Cord	Sanyo	2 Hours	$1,030

- Mutually Incompatible – Use Different Tape Materials, Recording Mechanisms, Formats
- Copyright Problems – Universal/Disney vs. Sony

VIDEO DISCS SYSTEMS

COMPANIES	PRINCIPLE	PLAYING TIME
Philips/MCA	Laser Optics	2 Hours
TED (Telefunken/Decca)	Piezo-Electric	10-15 Minutes
RCA	Capacitive	30 Minutes
Matsushita		2 Hours

- Inexpensive Pressed Vinyl Recordings
- Problems: The Tower of Babel; The Chicken and the Egg

THE FUNCTIONS OF STORAGE:

Store the Inputs	2, 3 (Data)
Store the Instructions	+, X (Program)
Store the Outputs	5, 6 (Data)
Store the Carrys	

DIGITAL COMPUTATION

Digits

		0	1	2	3	4	5	6
Decimal		0	1	2	3	4	5	6
Binary	000	001	010	011	100	101	110

Addition   DECIMAL   BINARY

$$
\text{Instruction} \longrightarrow
\begin{array}{r}
2 \leftarrow \text{Input} \\
+3 \leftarrow \text{Input} \\
\hline
=5 \leftarrow \text{Output}
\end{array}
\qquad
\text{Instruction}
\begin{array}{r}
010 \leftarrow \text{Input} \\
+011 \leftarrow \text{Input} \\
\hline
=101 \leftarrow \text{Output}
\end{array}
$$

Carry

MULTIPLICATION

$$
\begin{array}{r}
2 \\
\times 3 \\
\hline
6
\end{array}
\qquad
\begin{array}{r}
010 \\
\times 011 \\
\hline
010 \\
010 \\
\hline
00110
\end{array}
$$

```
                    ┌─────────────┐
                    │  ARITHMETIC │
                    │   (LOGIC)   │
                    └──────┬──────┘
                           ↑↓
┌─────────┐        ┌─────────────┐        ┌──────────┐
│  INPUT  │──────▶ │   STORAGE   │──────▶ │  OUTPUT  │
└─────────┘        │  (MEMORY)   │        └──────────┘
                   └──────┬──────┘
                          │
                          ├─ Carrys
                          ├─ Data
                          └─ Programs
```

OTHER TASKS OF DIGITAL COMPUTERS:

- Alphabet Can Be Coded Digitally
  Create Files (Airline Reservations, IRS, Etc.) and Retrieve, Search, Extract, Translate – From Them
- Images Can Be Described Digitally
  Represent Light Intensity and Color, Point by Point Across the field of an Image
- Sounds Can Be Recorded Digitally
  Represent Sound Intensity, Instant by Instant
- Communication Can Occur Between Computers, and with Dispersed Input and Output Equipments

ARCHIVAL MEMORY

What Is It?

- Large Volume ($>10^{15}$ Bits)
- On Line
- Rare Access to Data
- Very Inexpensive

Possible Technologies:

- Tapes and Film
- Video Discs
- Electron Microscope

Applications:

- Medical Data Bank
- Patent Office Files
- Library of Congress
- Social Security

Problems:

- How to Organize?

ON THE HORIZON:

- Mechanized Library
- Electronic Mail
- View Data

Beyond the Horizon:

- Inability to Organize
- Copyright Problems
- System Compatability
- Access to the World's Information
- New Foundation for Creativity

3 International Information Needs
Lynn W. Ellis

Of all activities in the communications process model, (exemplified in figure 3.1) only the transmission function is international in scope. While the information content of the other functions may be intended for international audiences, the generation activity takes place within national boundaries. It is the transmission function which crosses these boundaries, bringing with it opportunities and problems. This chapter will discuss international telecommunications technologies which facilitate the three bottom-most blocks in the diagram: <u>character</u>, <u>image</u>, and <u>voice</u> transmission. As the dominant form, voice transmission will be discussed first, and then the areas of image and data character. Finally, the chapter will discuss the current controversy about trans-border data-flows.

VOICE TRANSMISSION

Technologies for international transmission have traditionally been dominated by voice transmission, as two-way voice traffic represents some 90 percent of the total international traffic. Television is only 6 percent of international satellite traffic or about 3 percent of overall traffic.(1) The balance is data and character traffic. Thus, the real technical economic issue is what it costs each class of common carrier to obtain a voice circuit.

COMMUNICATION SATELLITE SYSTEMS AND COSTS

During John Kennedy's administration, it was decided that satellites were one of the coming modern technologies that would be relatively inexpensive, and would produce tremendous advantages in long-distance telecommunications.   The Communications Satellite Act of 1962 authorized the formation of the Communications Satellite Corporation (COMSAT).(2) COMSAT was authorized to participate as a carrier's carrier in the format of an International Satellite consortium (INTELSAT) to share this new technology with the whole world.(3) The promise at that time was that satellites were inexpensive and would supplant the submarine cables that had previously carried intercontinental traffic.(4) Unfortunately, history has shown a substantial gap between promise and performance.

For example, in 1973, an additional full circuit via the INTELSAT System from the United States to Europe cost the American Telephone and Telegraph or international record carrier (carriers authorized to serve end-users), over $50,000 per year.(5) At the same time the satellite proponents were saying, "a unit of utilization costs only about $8,500 per year, down from $20,000 in 1965."(6) These two statements have to be translated into equal terms. A unit of utilization covers the cost of a voice circuit one-way up to the satellite, and one-way back. Thus, for a full circuit, two units are required, for a total of nearly $17,000 a year.

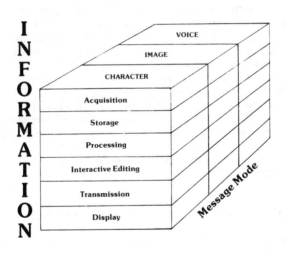

Fig. 3.1. A communication process model.

But the space segment isn't all of the cost. Two earth stations are also required, at a relatively fixed cost, independent of traffic. The Conference of European Post and Telecommunicating Administration (CEPT) has set a leased circuit tariff of 50,000 gold francs per year or a unit of utilization of one of the member countries' earth stations, equivalent to about $17,000 per year. COMSAT justified a 1975 tariff to the Federal Communications Commission (FCC) of $2,850 per month (or $34,200 per year) with the space segment included.(7) The total charge to the serving carrier at that time was over $50,000 for a full circuit across the Atlantic. The satellite costs were only about one-third of that total, and the ground station cost two-thirds.

That these costs are declining is a fact of modern technology. However, as of late 1979, while the space segment unit of utilization tariff is down to $5,760 per year, the European gold franc rate for the earth station has not changed, and as this must be paid in the destination country's currency, the amount has increased when reflected in the depreciated dollar. The 1979 COMSAT tariff of $1,340 per month ($16,080 per year) has also been reduced (space segment included). The total cost of the serving carrier is still of the order of $40,000 per circuit per year, but the satellite costs are now only one-quarter of that total.

One may well ask why the communication satellites that were supposed to be so cheap on the international scene came out so expensive in practice. First, the INTELSAT Consortium is a cost-plus-fixed-fee monopoly: They take the annual charges for operation of the system and add 14 percent pre-tax costs of capital, and divide the sum by the number of units of utilization – and that is the price of a unit.(8) The CEPT members are also in a monopoly position. Second, the charges suffer from the lack of an effective constraint or the level of investment, and the more invested, the higher the total return (the Averch-Johnson effect).(9) Even though the FCC regulates COMSAT's rate of return, the level of investment escapes control, as it is determined in the intergovernmental board of INTELSAT.(10)

Another factor related to over-investment is a decision of the INTELSAT Consortium to provide spare capacity to do all of its own restoral in the event of failure. This basically means that the system never runs more than half full. Since rarely in any of the three oceanic regions are more than two satellites in service at any one time, self restoration, without recourse to submarine cables, requires a maximum of 50 percent fill. The carrying cost of unused capacity is then passed along to the customer.(11)

COMPARISON WITH DOMESTIC SYSTEMS

Although INTELSAT initially provided service to Alaska, Hawaii, Puerto Rico, and many of the NASA space tracking stations around the world, the FCC has since authorized several domestic satellite systems. Freed from the rigidity of INTELSAT, and spurred by competition between themselves and land-line circuits, tariffs have been much lower than for international service. Typical rates have been in the range of $750 per month to $2,000 per month, according to distance as charges to the end-user. Since the carriers' filings to the FCC indicated revenue requirements of $12,000-15,000 per year per circuit, competition has clearly entailed some degree of marginal pricing.(12) This has been related to the low early fills (percent utilization), and the view that it is better to sell at below-revenue requirements than to leave the circuits idle until demand materialized. Even with this, satellites do not turn out to be a particularly inexpensive medium, because of the competition from long established land-line systems. A comparison made between ATT's filing for their domestic satellite system versus the equivalent land-line showed the break-even point to be at some 3,000 simultaneous circuits through the satellite, and at the same time, at distances above 1,500 miles.(13)

Submarine Cable Systems

One of the suppositions resulting from the implementation of telecommunications satellites was that there would be a dramatic reduction of submarine cables installed. This has been true in the United States because of governmental regulation rather than economics.(14) Economically, submarine cables have gone down rapidly in costs, at a faster rate than satellite tariffs.(15)

For example, the last two submarine cables installed across the Atlantic Ocean both had capital costs of about $40,000 a full circuit.(16) AT&T estimated estimated a revenue requirement per full circuit on TAT-6 (Transatlantic Telephone Cable No. 6) at $17,200 per annum.(17) Since operating and maintenance costs of a cable circuit are only about $1,000 per circuit-year, carriers with lower cost structures (and taxes) than AT&T would have had even lower revenue requirements, and to all the serving carriers this investment would have been appreciably more attractive than leasing from the INTELSAT Consortium at triple the price.

Naturally, all carriers (except COMSAT) were in favor of proceeding with a new submarine cable, TAT-7, under these favorable conditions. The Federal Communications Commission ruled that the marginal cost to the taxpaying public was zero because of excess satellite capacity, and delayed the commissioning of TAT-7 until mid-1983. Seeing its monopoly thus protected, INTELSAT then decided to put up even more investment in terms of the 1980 launch of INTELSAT V. The net result of this well-meaning government intervention is that the United States has fallen behind in commissioning submarine cables, and in obtaining the tariff benefits of their installation.

The rest of the world, on the other hand, has been more economically minded. In the four years 1974 through 1977, the capital cost of submarine systems, even with the restrictions of the FCC on systems landing in the United States, was $966 million.(18) During the same period, the capital cost of satellite systems was $556 million. So in effect, the submarine cables did not disappear.

For the longer term (1962-78), relative investment costs for submarine systems were $2 billion versus $1.8 billion for satellite systems.(19) However, these cables provided over 100,000 circuits, compared with about one-eighth this number in full satellite circuits. This cost ratio is one of the underlying reasons why submarine cable circuits are still in vogue around the world.

Short of a major change in FCC posture, it is doubtful that on the international scene there will be the benefit to the American user that has come from competition in domestic satellites or technological advances in submarine cables. But looking further out, the technology of fiber optics, with its potentially long spacings between repeaters (signal amplifies) and its light cable weight, make an ideal medium for submarine cables. In Japan and the United Kingdom, experiments on optical fiber submarine cables are underway. Given the lack of American government support to cables in the last half-decade, in decisions favoring satellites, it is doubtful that investment in submarine fiber optic technology will be made in the United States. Since other governments are investing in submarine cables, they will be the ones who reap the low-cost benefits of the application of optical fiber technology to submarine cable systems.

NEW SYSTEMS
Time-Assigned Speech Interpolation

What is in the technology being developed which may help this cost picture on the international scene? Time-Assigned Speech Interpolation (TASI) was originally developed by Bell Telephone Laboratories and is now in its fifth version (TASI-E). Up to the present, costs have not been coming down as fast as the underlying transmission media.

But the computer industries' progress with large scale integration has now shown the way towards miniaturization of TASI, with attendant reduction of costs. An advanced version for use by the carriers is now available from France.(20)

What is especially significant to the commercial user, however, is that a further miniaturized version is now available for installation on the customer's premises.(21) If a firm has five inter-continental circuits, an additional four are available through a mini-TASI at just $15,000 capital cost per circuit. If 16 circuits are available, an increment of 15 is available at $7,000 investment cost per circuit. Even at today's high interest rates, the annual charges for mini-TASI are well below international tariffs for additional circuits. Thus, the technological developments derived from the computer industry are leading to time-assigned speech interpolation being probably the most cost-effective way of living with the expensive circuit tariffs being found on the international scene.

INTERNATIONAL RECORD (NON-VOICE) TELECOMMUNICATIONS

Communications other than voice are designated in regulatory proceedings as record communications. These involve traditional character transmission (message telegrams, telex), data transmission between computers and/or terminals, and image transmission.

Character transmission

The sum of character and data transmission traffic internationally is in the range of 7-10 percent of the total traffic. The two are electrically equivalent, being expressed in terms of the presence or absence of an electrical signal. Only the coding of the resulting impulses separates character from data transmission, although the terminal equipment is quite distinct.

A quite old technology of voice-frequency carrier telegraphy (VFCT) has been used to move character (telegraph) signals over voice circuits, by substituting the on-off electrical signal for an on-off tone (AM) or more recently by the shift of tone frequency (FM or FsK). Thus, practically all character transmission has long since been transferred to voice circuits with 18 character (telegraph) circuits per voice circuit in the United States, or up to 24 telegraph circuits per voice circuit internationally. When data came along first at low speeds, the same technology was used for data.

One of the reasons the character area has not moved faster is that traditional pricing dated back to the time when there were only telegraph circuits. The first of these had been a single wire with earth return. When the telephone arrived, two wires were required because the earth return was too noisy. Therefore, the telephone circuit was twice the price of the telegraph circuit, or the latter was half the price of the former. In many countries of Europe, this is still today the pricing policy nationally, while internationally a telegraph circuit tariff is in the range of one-quarter to one-third a voice circuit. With a technology which gives up to 24 telegraph circuits to the voice circuit, the cost of the VFCT adaptors is easily repaid out of such high tariffs. Yet the traditionalism of this area long held back reducing tariffs to marginal costs, thus slowing the growth of character transmission.

Data transmission

With the advent of data transmission, speeds higher than the traditional 50 bits per second of carrier telegraphy were required. Parallel tone transmission proved less economic than a single tone with a wider frequency shift. First 1,200, then 2,400 bits per second were obtained this way from a voice circuit. Now more sophisticated modulation techniques have pushed this limit up to 9,600 bits per second. Time division multiplexing techniques have now enabled 192 telegraph circuits to use a single voice circuit, yet tariffs have not kept pace. Even for data purposes, tariff surcharges are traditional for many services about 1,200 bits per second, holding an umbrella over telegraph tariffs.

With satellite circuits, it is now possible to obtain a 56-kilobits-per-second data circuit from a single voice circuit. The only problem is that there is an accompanying time delay. This is because the signal must go 23,000 miles up to the satellite, and the same distance back, and this delay of about one-quarter of a second each way puts the computer on waiting time. As a consequence about 80 percent of the requests for data circuits are for installation via submarine cables, because the customer finds that he is not able to accept that sort of time delay on his computer system.

Simultaneous voice-data and alternative voice-data circuits are offered by the international record carriers, where the circuit is used for voice and data at the same time, or alternately. Alternate use makes a lot of sense in international telecommunication because of time zone differences. The period of work-hour overlap between New York and London business offices is only from 9 to 12 noon New York time. The remainder of the day, the circuit can be used for data communications with the total cost of the alternate voice-data circuit only a few thousand dollars per year above that of a single purpose circuit.

Image transmission

As mentioned earlier, image transmission on the international scene is today only some 3 percent of the total. It would not be that high today if it were not for the adventurous 180-unit of utilization lease by Spain and Mexico of a transponder in June 1972 for a continuous 24-hour Spanish language television service to Latin America.(22) At that time this use provided about half the INTELSAT image traffic. With Mexico dropping out in March, 1976, Spain took over the lease and has continued it for service aimed principally at their domestic provinces in the Canary Island, and secondarily at Latin America. The balance of INTELSAT use is occasioned, heavily influenced by major sporting events (World Soccer Cup, Olympics, etc.).

One of the limitations of image transmission is that a picture is really worth a thousand words, and costs about that much more to transmit in real time than a voice circuit. Thus, the rate quoted above for the Spanish lease is marginal pricing, and yet is still too high to provide an economic incentive for greater use of the service. Non-real time transmission is quite possible at less band width – facsimile uses just a voice circuit with a delay of six minutes to the page for the least sophisticated terminal.

An in-between technology is being developed in Europe and Canada for two services: one-way teletext (character transmission on home television sets) and two-way view data (interactive character transmission on television sets).(23) Teletext uses the fly-back time (a blanked-out time between the end of one line and the start of the next) of the television picture to insert a communication one-way from the broadcast station to the house television receiver. An integrated circuit decoder (a multitransistor semiconductor device or "chip") selects one of up to one hundred pages in response to the selection on a dial by the recipient. This service is being sponsored by governments in other countries and is being quietly resisted by commercial broadcasting advertisers in this country, who naturally do not want user diversion from the high-priced commercials for which they have paid.

The view-data service uses the same format on the video screen, but an associated telephone line and data transmission modem (modulator or converter from digital to analog signals – demodulator or converter from analog to digital signals) brings access via a menu selection approach to up to 200,000 pages of data. The French have a system called ANTIOPE, the English have one called PRESTEL, and the West Germans are trying a German language version of PRESTEL. In this case, the user doesn't get a free service as he does from teletext. He has to pay the terminal charge for the modem and television set, the usage charge for the distance to the source computer, and for the pages used to the provider of the data base.

TRANS-BORDER DATA FLOW

The final subject of this chapter concerns trans-border data flow. An example will be given of an ambitious system devised by one manufacturing company.   The accompanying national economic and privacy problems will also be reviewed.

The industrial data network used as an example in this instance is that of the Fairchild Camera and Instrument Corporation.(24) This company makes a wide range of semiconductor products, from discrete units through integral circuits. It has a large organization in the United States and in Europe, is headquartered in Mountainview, California, and maintains principal factories in Singapore and Hong Kong. Thus, the company operates in three almost equally separated time zones, with minimal overlaps of working hours.

At one time, Fairchild operated its network with each location having a separate computer. Later, location messages were by standard telex (character) switched services. Orderflow meant a message to the appropriate factory, replied to or by shipping notice, with additional copies to headquarters for billing. During the period of this distributed transactional operation, inventories averaged 40 percent of sales.

A new network was devised based on alternate voice-data circuits. On Mountainview time, the overlap to New York is from 9 A.M.-noon to 2 P.M., the overlap to Europe is briefly around 9 A.M., and the overlap to the Far East is briefly around 5 P.M. for the late stayers at the office and the early risers in the Orient. A similar low overlap exists between Europe and the Far East. Typically, each circuit is used for voice purposes two hours per day; the rest of the time it is configured for data. Each location now has only a remote job-entry terminal instead of the previous computer, with a master computer at Mountainview. On the average each circuit handles five to six hours of data per day. The orders go to Mountainview, the production scheduling is done from Mountainview, the shipping instructions go to the Far East where products are shipped directly to destination, and the billing is issued from Mountainview, often back over the same alternate voice-data circuit to be printed at the far end. Fairchild's semiconductor division is now running just over 10 percent inventory to sales ratio on the new system. This is a saving to the company in investment of 30 percent per year.

ECONOMIC PROBLEMS FROM AN OVERSEAS VIEWPOINT

What the company is saving in such an international data network is often seen, particularly in developing countries, as their economic loss. The computers which are made in Europe and Japan are no longer being purchased for the overseas locations. The skilled programmer/analyst teams which prepared software are also no longer needed, since one less-skilled operator can handle a remote job-entry terminal. Cutting into employment is a cardinal sin in many countries, particularly when it takes away opportunities for skilled workers. Several countries have laws making layoffs under such conditions economically prohibitive.

Privacy Regulations

It is not surprising that many international executives see the sudden spurt of privacy regulations, particularly in Europe, as an indirect restraint on establishing economic data networks of the type here discussed. The European Economic Community, however, steadfastly maintains that these regulations are not pointed against multi-national businesses.(25) Their view is that the web of regulations is a natural result of independent national parliaments attempting to protect the individual against potential infringements of his privacy.

Not only is personnel data involved in these regulations, but also effectively in business privacy. For example, when a Swedish motor car manufacturer orders Fairchild semiconductors for its automobile controls, that order book is now accessible on the other side of the world in California. In the event that links are not secure (many countries monitor others' satellite circuits), the state of the order book is available elsewhere also. A company such as FCI has many types of information which local privacy regulations would preclude from being handled on its international data network.

SUMMARY AND CONCLUSIONS

This paper has briefly covered the technological background of international transmission of voice, character and image information and some problems of trans-border data flows.

Some interesting conclusions result. First, despite a steady stream of complementary public relations information emanating from the satellite industry, their international economic performance has fallen far short of initial promise and of competitive media, such as submarine cables. With the present mood for deregulation, one of the actions which would save most money for international telecommunication users would be total deregulation leading to price competition in international communications. The present trend of government intervention in the United States has not been effective economically.

Second, the tariff structure for data, based on ancient wisdom from telegraphy, favors economies of scale in data. That is, doing what Fairchild has done and operating one central worldwide service via alternate voice-data links.

A third conclusion is that because of the social problems and consequent regulation of trans-border data flows, and because of the natural tendency of the human race to verbalize, voice is still going to dominate the international scene through the 1980s.

Finally, in my view, all users of communications have to speak softly, but firmly, at every opportunity on the subject of the regulation of trans-border data flow. It is in the user community's interest to keep regulation to the extent that it controls only abuses and does not restrict economic progress in international telecommunications.

NOTES

(1) Marcellus S. Snow, International Commercial Satellite Communications: Economic and Political Issues at the Decade of Intelsat, New York: Praeger, 1976, p. 53. See also his Ph.D. dissertation, University of California at Berkeley, 1974.

(2) U.S. Congress, An Act to Provide for Re-Establishment, Ownership, and Regulation of a Commercial Communications Satellite System and For Other Purposes, Public Law 62F, 87th Congress, 2nd Session, August 31, 1962.

(3) Snow, Satellite Communications, pp. 3-11.

(4) U.S. National Academy of Engineering, Reports on Selected Topics in Telecommunications (Washington, 1969); U.S. President 1965-68 (Johnson), Task Force on Communications Policy, Summary Report (Washington: GPO, June, 1969).

(5) The tariffs to the end user are much higher, reflecting the embedded costs of older facilities, and the costs from the gateway to the user's premises. In other words, the end user pays average annual costs plus overheads and profit. The discussion in this paper, however, is in terms of annual marginal costs of incremental capacity to the serving carrier either from its own investment or lease from the carrier's carriers (COMSAT and INTELSAT).

(6) Snow, Satellite Communications, p. 90.

(7) Joseph N. Pelton, and Marcellus S. Snow, eds., Economic and Policy Problems in Satellite Communications (N.Y.: Praeger, 1977), p. 26.

(8) Snow, Satellite Communications, p. 23.

(9) Harvey Averch, and Leland L. Johnson, "Behavior of the Firm Under Regulatory Constraint," American Economic Review 52 (December 1962), pp. 1053-1069.

(10) Samuel A. Maddelena, "The Management of International Telecommunications: A Study of the Role of U.S. Government Regulation," Ph.D. dissertation, Pace University, 1979.

(11) The current U.S.-United Kingdom end-user per circuit is $107,400 per year (plus $8,658 UK value-added tax), reflecting all of the inefficiencies discussed and costs noted in footnote 4 above.

(12) Wilbur C. Prichard, et al, Communications Satellite Systems Worldwide, 1975-1985 (Dedham, Mass.: Horizon House, 1975).

(13) Lynn W. Ellis, "Economies of Scale in Telecommunications: Analysis, Strategies, Management," Ph.D. dissertation, Pace University, 1978.

(14) Maddelena, "International Telecommunications."

(15) Bogumil M. Dawidziuk, and H.F. Preston, "International Communications: Network Developments and Economics," Proceedings of the 3rd World Telecommunication Forum (Geneva: International Telecommunication Union, 1979), pp. 3.411.1-14.

(16) U.S. Dept. of Commerce, Office of Telecommunications, The World's Submarine Telephone Cable Systems, OT (Contractor Report 75-7, Washington, August, 1975, Referring to CANTAT-2, 1974, and TAT-6, 1976).

(17) Pelton and Snow, Economic and Policy Problems, p. 80.

(18) Bogumil M. Dawidziuk, "Recent Development in the Global Submarine Systems Network," Proceedings of INTELCOM-79, (Dedham, Ma.: Horizon House, 1979).

(19) Dawidziuk and Preston, "International Communications," pp. 3, 4, 11.9.

(20) "Celtic Telephone Channel Speech Concentrator" [brochure] (Paris: CIT-Alcatel, 1979).

(21) C.E. White, "Bits of Voice," Telecommunications 12 (April, 1978); "Com-2," [brochure] (Broomfield, Colorado: Storage Technology Corporation, 1979).

(22) Pelton and Snow, Economic and Policy Problems, p. 20.

(23) Samuel Fedida, "View Data Developments in the United Kingdom"; P. Ledercq, "The Introduction of Videotex Services in France"; B.P. Nicholls et al, "A Videotex Development in Canada," Proceedings of the 3rd World Telecommunication Forum (Geneva: International Communication Union, 1979).

(24) "Economics of an Industrial Data Network," paper presented at Intelcom '79, Dallas, Texas.

(25) Edmund F.M. Hogrebe, "International Data Regulation Issues from the Perspective of the European Economic Community," Proceedings of Intelcom '79 (Dedham, Ma.: Horizon House, 1979), pp. 194-196.

4 Satellite Communications
B.H. Burdine

One of the most significant early benefits from the space age has been the development and use of communications satellites. Many aspects of national and international business have been affected, and to some extent the daily lives of people everywhere have benefitted. In terms of major projects carried out on a worldwide scale, the payoff from satellites has been rapid.

At this writing, it is just a decade-and-a-half since the first commercial communication satellite was launched into synchronous orbit, and only a quarter-century since Arthur C. Clarke, then a relatively unknown engineer working for the British Post Office, proposed the idea of using three geosynchronous (i.e., stationary) satellites, powered by solar energy, to provide worldwide communications. In 1955 Clarke and John Pierce of Bell Labs, both of them practical visionaries, made further technical proposals that would lead ultimately to the extensive network of satellites and earth stations we have today. What had attracted Pierce's attention was that the 36-channel transatlantic cable then being laid would cost $35 million, and he felt that a satellite with 30 times the capacity would probably be a better solution, although one having higher initial cost. Indeed he was right; we now know that a COMSTAR satellite launched in 1976 at a cost of about $65 million carries 36,000 half-circuits (that is, 18,000 phone calls at one time).

INTELSAT SERIES

The first INTELSAT satellite weighing 38 kg (about 80 pounds), carried 240 phone circuits. It had a design life of 1½ years. Successive satellites in the INTELSAT series (shown in figure 4.1) had greater weight, and longer life expectancy. The latest of the series now in use is INTELSAT IV, shown in figure 4.1. It has a capacity of

6,000 circuits and weighs 830 kg. It is designed to last seven years and will probably last longer.

Why single out satellites among the many forms of transmission? Why are they so special? Probably the most unusual feature of a satellite communication link is that its cost is independent of the distance between end points, provided both ends can receive a signal from the same satellite. Also the link performance does not depend on the terrain in between. That feature alone has allowed many developing countries (for example, Algeria and Nigeria) to install "instant long lines" networks without the difficult task of putting cable or microwave towers across the mountains or deserts. It allows additional circuits from Hawaii and Europe to continental United States without laying additional undersea cable.

Any location within the typical "footprint" or coverage pattern shown in figure 4.2 can in theory communicate with any other location. There are practical considerations and problems that limit this kind of operation, if dependable, high quality links are to be implemented.

Synchronous satellites of the INTELSAT system are in orbit over the Indian, Atlantic, and Pacific Oceans; and just as Arthur Clarke suggested, they provide essentially worldwide coverage. Russia operates a system of low altitude satellites in highly elliptical non-synchronous orbits to cover the northern reaches of that country.

Frequency Sharing

An interesting thing about the eleven INTELSAT satellites and ten others in the American and Canadian domestic system is that they all operated in a shared 4/6 GHz (for Gigahertz) frequency band. The uplinks operated near 6 GHz and the downlinks near 4 GHz. The frequencies are allocated by international agreements having the force of treaties between members of the International Consultative Radio Committee (CCIR). They are set by a World Administrative Radio Committee (WARC) whose actions establish policy for the next twenty years following each meeting.

The rather complex chart of figure 4.3 shows the 500 MHz-wide uplink and downlink allocations which are further sub-divided into channels. Each channel can carry 1,000 to 1,500 voice circuits or one or two TV signals. Each satellite of the latest design can operate on all these subchannels at once. All earth stations and satellites must be designed to avoid the possibility of mutual interference. This problem is complicated when one considers that most of the microwave radio towers spread across the country with six- or eight-foot parabolic antennas or horns on them also work on the same frequency assignments.

Figure 4.4 is a plot of these so-called line-of-sight microwave links operating in Florida on the downlink 4-GHz frequency band, showing how extensive that terrestrial network really is. Since all these stations are operating in the same frequency band, they can perform satisfactorily only if they are designed not to interfere with each other.

DOMESTIC SATELLITES

Figure 4.5 illustrates the relative position of the ten synchronous-orbit satellites of the United States and Canadian domestic systems. Five of these satellites (two used by RCA and three by AT&T/GTE) have 24 transponders each, that is, they make use of all the allocated sub-channels while the remaining five satellites have only 12 transponders each. Note the spacing of around 5 degrees between adjacent satellites. This is necessary to prevent an earth station from illuminating or "seeing" two satellites at the same time and creating interference in the one not intended for use.

Earth Stations

To achieve the narrow beam necessary for communicating with these satellites, very large antennas are used. The GTE station in Hawaii as shown in figure 4.6 is the standard 32-meter size used for major stations. Its very narrow pencil beam assures that it "sees" only one satellite at a time. You may remember from your science courses that the larger reflector of a big spotlight creates a smaller beam of light at a greater distance. It is the same with these antennas.

Most domestic earth stations, such as the GTE Station at Homosassa, Florida (shown in figure 4.7), use two antennas. Why two? Do we expect this large multimillion dollar structure to fail? No, but we do have to provide essentially continuous service, which means providing for those times when the earth station experiences sun transit or when it is necessary to switch to a standby satellite.

NEW TECHNIQUES

Sun Transit

Sun transit is a term used to describe the few minutes per day in spring and fall when for a few days the sun appears to cross directly behind the satellite as shown in figure 4.8. The sun, an obvious source of very intense light, is also a source of very intense noise in the frequency bands of the satellites. During sun transit, the circuits may become very noisy, and to maintain acceptable service all traffic is switched over to the standby satellite. In this way it is possible to avoid a circuit outage that is entirely predictable. Since the design goal for a satellite common carrier is for an outage of less than one hour per year from all causes, eliminating this predictable outage helps to assure that goal is met. The standby satellite is also available for backup in the unlikely event the main satellite should fail.

Orbit Crowding

Now what happens when all useful orbital "parking places" that can be "seen" by domestic North American earth stations are filled? Assuming the satellites are packed as tight as possible and that Canada and perhaps some South American countries have placed added satellites in orbit, two things can be done. By making each satellite "illuminate" only part of the continent, rather than the whole, as at present (see figure 4.2), it is possible to double the in-orbit capacity. (That is being done with INTELSAT V, launched in 1980.) However, another promising technique is to add a new set of satellites working in a different frequency band and interspersed among those already in orbit. This is equivalent to the way a TV station, say channel 2, can put a UHF antenna, say channel 44, on the same tower and operate both stations simultaneously. The TV viewer can pick either or both stations. They can carry different programs, but they do not interfere with each other. INTELSAT V also makes use of this technique by carrying equipment working in two different frequency bands.

New Frequency Bands

At present, three frequency bands are allocated for use by communication satellites as shown in figure 4.9. The 4/6-GHz band currently in use employs well-developed technology. The other bands have been used experimentally. Both have advantages. Chief among these is the possibility of using small, inexpensive rooftop antennas. A purely technical advantage of great importance to the system designer is the absence of interference from terrestrial microwave links that is so prevalent in the currently-used 4/6 GHz bands.

These higher frequencies are called K-band, and you will be hearing a good deal more about them in the future. At K-band frequencies no serious source of terrestrial interference now exists. Due to characteristics of system design and signal propagation in the higher bands, interference problems would never be as severe as they are in the 4/6 GHz bands. A typical K-band earth station antenna is shown in figure 4.10. In view of the advantages of using a small rooftop antenna such as this, why would one not want to move immediately into K-band operation? From the equipment point of view, there has been a natural evolution from the well-developed 4/6 GHz terrestrial networks of the 1950s to satellite systems of the 1970s using the same equipment and a mature technology. The history of all radio communication has generally been one of pushing into higher bands to gain added capacity. Equipment for K-band satellites and earth stations is now reaching acceptable levels of performance and reliability for use in new systems.

Rain Effects

While operation at K-band has many advantages, there is one significant problem that must be overcome or accommodated. That is the effect of heavy rain on signal propagation.

Suppose we are operating our 12/14-GHz K-band station at GTE Laboratories in Waltham, Massachusetts, when a rainstorm approaches from the southwest, as it often does. Our signal must go through the rain cloud as shown in figure 4.11, and it will be severely disturbed when the rain is heavy.

The effect is similar to what would happen if you try to use a flashlight in a downpour. The light becomes scattered, weakened, and entirely lost after a short distance. To overcome the loss you could use a larger flashlight or a spotlight, and by analogy the earth station and the satellite can be made more powerful, but there are technical and economic limits on just how far one can go. There are other possibilities, however, and they are being explored by Bell Labs, GTE Labs, and other experimenters.

The map of figure 4.12 shows why rain effects must be taken into account. Much of the eastern half of the United States experiences heavy rainstorms during a typical year. These contours, prepared by Bell Labs, show that based on New Jersey as a reference, the Gulf Coast is five to six times more likely to have a rainstorm of one inch per hour or greater. In fact the Tampa area experiences 89 thunderstorm days in an average year. Connecticut should have fewer than ten.

If these storms are examined in detail, it becomes clear that the very heavy rain does not generally occur over a very large area at the same time. For example, people often observe a downpour in the middle of the causeway between Tampa and St. Petersburg while no rain is falling at either side.

To further understand the make-up of the storms and their effect on satellite signals, we have installed three rooftop earth stations in the Tampa area. Figure 4.13 shows one of these antennas located at the University of South Florida. Note how small the antenna is when compared to the large station at Homosassa. It is only 2.5 meters in diameter. Similar antennas are located on the rooftops of two General Telephone of Florida telephone offices about 8 miles away. The three stations each receive 19/29 GHz test signals from the COMSTAR satellites used jointly by AT&T and GTE. By comparing the signals received at the three stations, we can determine which is least affected by the rain at any given instant and choose that one. This is called diversity operation. Our data for two years of operation shows that by using two such stations (not three) we could achieve acceptable system performance.

You will recall that current stations typically have two large antennas to handle the sun transit problem by using two satellites. In future K-band stations we could simply separate the two smaller antennas by eight or ten miles and handle sun transit as well as diversity operation to overcome the rain outages.

While GTE Labs, Bell Labs, and others are now collecting data at 19/29 GHz, the effects of rain at 12/14 GHz have also been measured, and as theory predicted, the effect is less severe. Several sets of data have been collected from ATS satellites and from the Joint Canadian-U.S. satellite called CTS. However, the outage from rain, even in the

Boston area where we have made our tests, would still require diversity operation to achieve telephone network performance standards of less than one hour per year total outage.

Our record of a single rain event in August 1977 (figure 4.14) shows that the signal at Waltham dropped to 10 percent of its normal value for over 20 minutes. In the absence of a diversity station, this fade would have caused loss of communication for 25 minutes or more. From the rain map shown earlier, we could predict that the Gulf Coast would have ten times as many events of this severity, while other areas would fall in between these two.

Future Systems

What does all this say about operation of future satellite systems in the higher frequency bands? Certainly a general purpose common carrier satellite system such as those operated by GTE and AT&T would require diversity stations in much of the eastern United States, and in some other places in the country depending on local conditions, unless the required system margin can be achieved in some other way.

For private line services such as data, electronic mail, or video conferencing, the second station could perhaps be eliminated if longer and more frequent outages can be tolerated. In some areas, however, ten to twenty hours of outage could be expected for a single station in an average year.

SUPER-SATELLITES

Finally, I would like to comment on proposed super-satellites of the future and the services they might provide.

Figure 4.15 is a photograph of the INTELSAT V satellite launched in 1980. The trend has been toward bigger satellites (INTELSAT V weighs 4,000 pounds) and where possible, smaller earth stations. (The GTE Labs Triad antennas working at 19/29 GHz are only 2.5 meters in diameter.) INTELSAT V and other planned satellites have transponders at 4/6 GHZ and one or both of the K-bands as well on the same satellite.

How far will this trend go?

Futuristic Satellites

The super-satellite shown in figure 4.16 is an idea resulting from a NASA study. It would weigh 54,000 pounds, carry a voice switch with twice the capacity of the largest Bell System electronic switch in existence today and would employ 7,000 antenna beams, each aimed toward a region of the country only 30 to 60 miles in size.

Ivan Bekey describes the idea in the February 1979 issue of Astronautics and Aeronautics. The system could allow 25 million users to communicate by a "Dick Tracy" wrist telephone.

The satellite could alternatively be used for electronic mail connecting 500,000 offices, each with a rooftop antenna similar to the one used in the GTE Labs Tampa Triad. It could also provide educational TV for 80,000 schools, or video conferencing from 500 studios.

All of this assumes a highly sophisticated discipline of timed access by the earth stations and the successful operation of a complex satellite larger than any ever constructed. It uses 7,000 non-interfering beams from a 200-foot antenna precisely aimed so that each beam covers a separate area. Will satellite communications evolve toward this kind of "super system"? The technology will certainly be available in the 1980s and we can be fairly certain the satellites will be larger and the earth stations smaller. The possible economic and societal effects of such advances are much less certain. What we can hope to do is make it easier, quicker, and less expensive for anyone who wants to convey a message, and hope that Henry David Thoreau was wrong when he observed in Walden, "our inventions are wont to be. . . improved means to an unimproved end. . . . "

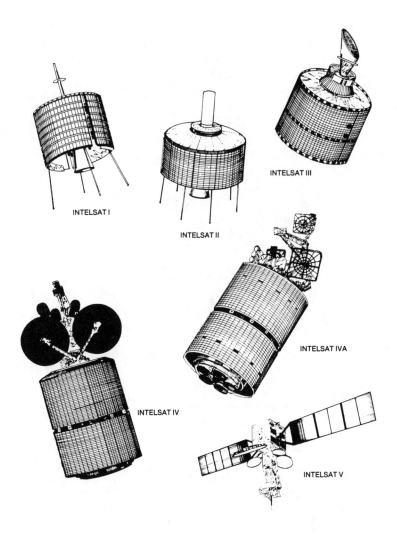

Fig. 4.1. Satellites in the INTELSAT series.

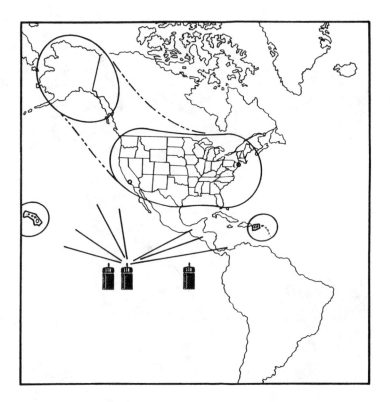

Fig. 4.2. Coverage pattern of COMSTAR satellites. Any location within the "footprint" or coverage pattern can in theory communicate with any other location.

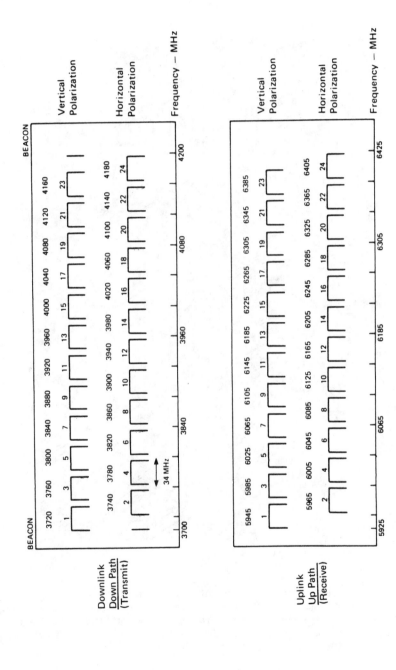

Fig. 4.3. Channel allocation in the 4/6-GHz frequency bands.

43

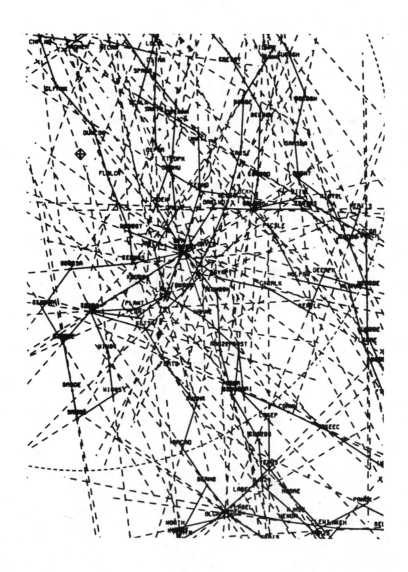

Fig. 4.4. Florida microwave link map – 4 GHz. This is a plot of the so-called line-of-sight microwave links operating in Florida, showing how extensive that terrestrial network is. Since all these stations are operating in the same frequency band, they can only perform satisfactorily if they are designed not to interfere with each other.

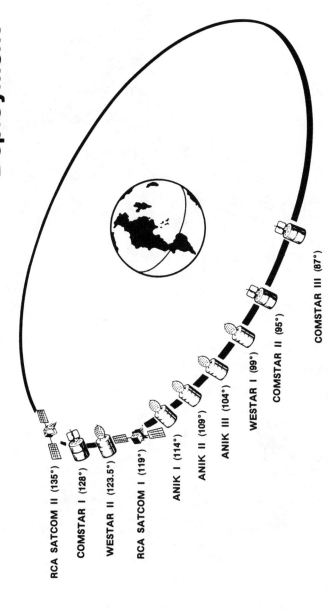

DOMESTIC SATELLITE
Deployment

RCA SATCOM II (135°)
COMSTAR I (128°)
WESTAR II (123.5°)
RCA SATCOM I (119°)
ANIK I (114°)
ANIK II (109°)
ANIK III (104°)
WESTAR I (99°)
COMSTAR II (95°)
COMSTAR III (87°)

Fig. 4.5. Satellites providing North American domestic service: ANIK – Canadian; WESTAR – Western Union; SATCOM – RCA American; COMSTAR – AT&T/GTE.

Fig. 4.6. GTE earth station in Hawaii.

Fig. 4.7. GTE earth station in Homosassa, Florida.

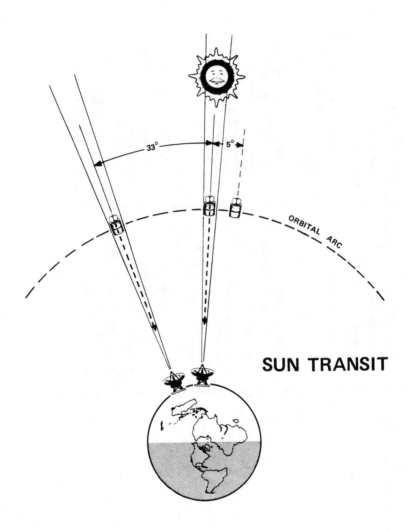

Fig. 4.8. Sun transit.

FREQUENCY (GHz)	ADVANTAGES	DISADVANTAGES
4/6	• Technology Exists • Frequency Re—Use by Orthogonal Polarization • Rain Effects are Small	• Large Antennas • Sites Very Limited (Terrestrial Interference) • Faraday Rotation Correction Needed for Frequency Re—Use (Polarization)
12/14	• Rooftop Antennas • Short or No Back—Haul Needed • Spot Beams • No Faraday Rotation Correction Required • On—Board Signal Processing and Beam Switching (Future)	• Rain Effects are Significant • Diversity Stations May Be Required in Certain Regions • Frequency Re—Use by Orthogonal Polarization May Be Difficult or Limited
18/30	• 2.5 GHz Bandwidth Available • Spot Beams, Beam Switching • Small Antennas • No Faraday Rotation Correction Required • No Back—Haul Needed	• Satellite May Require High Power • Rain Effects are Very Significant • Diversity Stations Required in Most Regions • Frequency Re—Use by Orthogonal Polarization May Be Impossible • Bandwidth Limitations Unknown

Fig. 4.9. Communication satellite frequency bands.

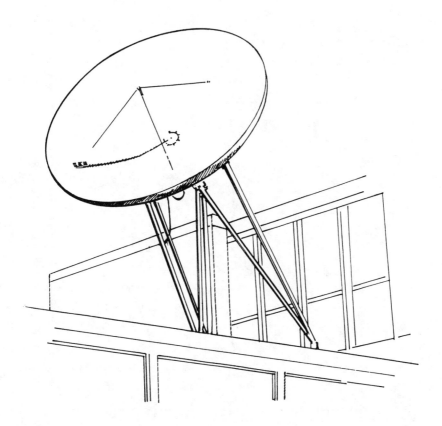

Fig. 4.10. 3-meter rooftop antenna for the 12/14-GHz band.

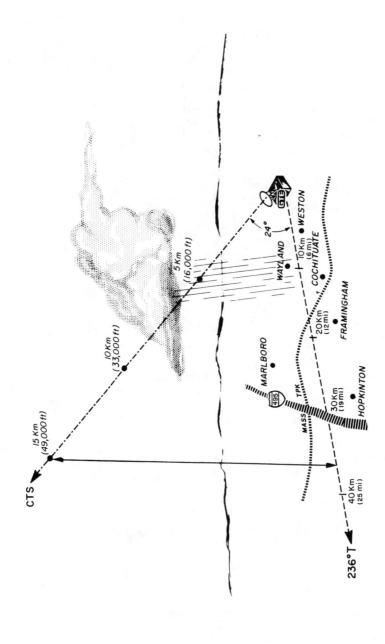

Fig. 4.11. Signal path through a rainstorm. A signal will be severely disturbed when the rain is heavy. The effect is similar to what would happen if you try to use a flashlight in a downpour. The light becomes scattered, weakened, and entirely lost after a short distance.

50

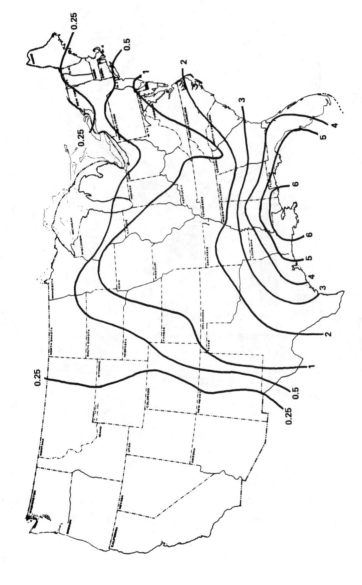

Fig. 4.12. Curves of equal rainfall incidence (the Florida Gulf Coast has more than 80 thunderstorms per year). Source: Dyck & Mattice, Mon. Wea. Rev. 69 (1941) as adapted by H.W. Evans, Bell Labs.

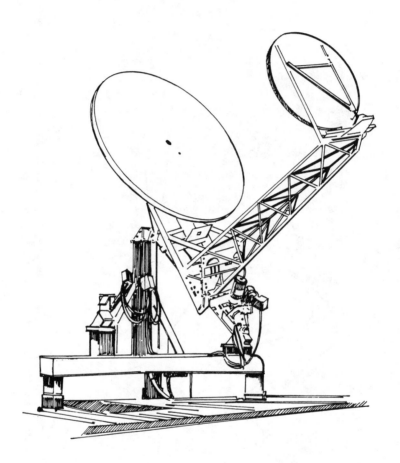

Fig. 4.13. 19/29-GHz rooftop antenna.

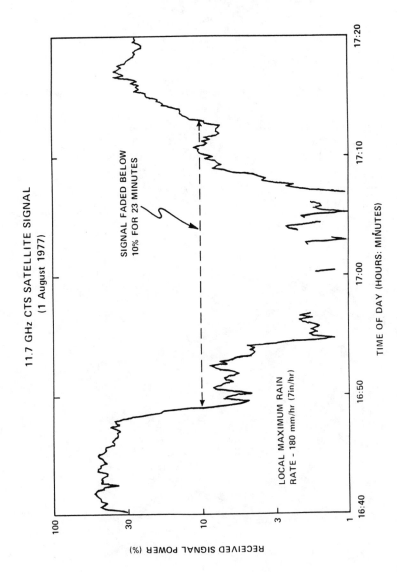

Fig. 4.14. Rain fade at Waltham, Massachusetts. During a single rain event in August 1977, the signal at Waltham dropped to 10 percent of its normal value.

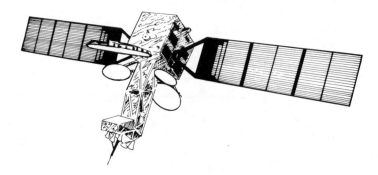

Fig. 4.15. INTELSAT V satellite.

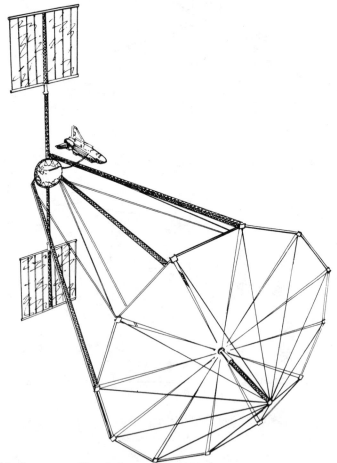

Fig. 4.16. Super satellite being serviced by space shuttle.

5 The New Generation of Graphics in the Information Business

Richard J. Hayes

I will discuss graphics in the information business, from a technologist's perspective. What do we mean by the information business, what do we mean by graphics, and what technologies are we discussing? Let me list five technological steps that cover everything in the information business: creation, processing, communications, filing, and reproduction. You can spend a lot of time thinking about different processes, and if you come up with one that can't be handled under these headings, I would be glad to talk to you. One of the first questions someone asked was on interactive displays. I said, "Fine, but that is just a combination of processing and reproducing." So, in my world we drop everything into five buckets, and talk about the different applications of technologies.

I would like to focus a bit further on information and graphics in the office environment, and the office of the future. I think that the easiest way to start is to consider the changes that have occurred in the office. Basically, we have had: electronic typewriting since the 1940s; dictating in the 1950s; convenience copying in the early 1960s; computers since the 1950s and 1960s; word processing in the 1970s. In the 1980s we predict that it will be broad-band communications. We have had lots of discussion about automated factories and automated processes, but now the office is starting to come into focus.

In 1977 we did a survey of articles about manufacturing productivity and worker productivity in the factories. Since Frederick W. Taylor's time in the early 1900s, there have been over 10,000 such studies. But when we catalogued serious studies of office productivity, we found only about 300. There are many more now, by the way, and they are starting to roll out in every publication you pick up. You can understand why these studies are multiplying if you take a look at how in the United States, the office labor force is growing — as opposed to manufacturing, where it's stable — and how labor costs are going up. A couple of years ago the cost was rising at a rate of 8 percent and now it is higher.

55

Despite these many recent studies of office productivity, actual productivity per worker is going down. When you look at the capital investment in the equipment per worker, you find that in the manufacturing areas, these costs amount to an average of $25,000 per worker, whereas in the office the average is $2,000 (see table 5.1). To increase productivity and hold the costs down, more capital will be spent per worker in the office environment over the next several years. Much of this increase will go for technology. It will be used to improve productivity, to shorten the response time necessary to get information processed, to upgrade the quality of information flow – and still contain costs.

The reason for office changes and the introduction of newer techniques is to improve the generation and revision of information, its printing and reproduction, distribution and communication, and filing and retrieval. But one has to make these new systems friendly, with the office employees in mind, so that they augment people's normal way of doing things. You don't revolutionize the whole process, as some people have found out the hard way.

I would like to stress, however, that from our point of view the office of the future is now emerging. It is in a process of evolutionary change; we are not going to wait and wake up one day in 1985 and say we are now in the office of the future. Things that are changing as we look ahead are: the systemized flow of information in the office; obtaining better equipment and better processes to handle the flow of information; and (coming from Xerox it may seem strange) we see paper playing a role, albeit a different role. We really don't see a paperless office. Many of the intermediate steps where people now use paper will be processed in digital form. Again, I stress the point that it will be an evolutionary change, not a revolution.

Table 5.1. UNITED STATES

ADMINISTRATION		MANUFACTURING
GROWING	LABOR FORCE	STABLE
8%	ANNUAL COST INCREASE	6%
4%	ANNUAL PRODUCTIVITY INCREASE	9%
$2000	PER CAPITA CAPITAL INVESTMENT	$25,000

Let me pick up some of the evidence of the changes that have happened. The typewriter is now blending into word processing. On the reproduction end, all of the steps involved with composition, setup, and make-ready are now possible with automated reproduction and a combination of certain word processing equipment. One of the major trends is: impact printing or character printing, involving people, typewriters, band printers, and chain printers, is giving way to non-impact printing. There are many reasons for this major change. Pre-press operations are becoming automated. Most enterprises find that in their flow of information they have to communicate with somebody else, and most products are put into the market with the capability of talking with some other product. We used to think of data processing as being hidden somewhere in the building, and we regarded it as different from the administrative operations in the same building. But data processing and administrative operations are now merging. While all these things are going on, the same steps take place – generation, revision, distribution, filing, and retrieval.

Let's take a look at the technology trends in those steps, and get an idea of the kinds of products and the things that are happening in each area. Let us go back to our favorite five steps and talk about stand-alone products. Each one of those areas has stand-alone products in them, and each has a function. On the other hand, integrated systems with a combination of one or more of those steps, are also evolving.

We talk about the three different modes, character, image, and voice (see figure 5.1). I want to focus on the image: the image, meaning graphics, in each one of those steps, as opposed to capturing and processing character or voice code information. We want to talk about what we in our world call imaginal or non-keystroke captured data. As one looks down each of those steps and reflects a bit, one comes to the conclusion that graphics are really involved in all phases of the information business and are an important part of the office environment.

Let me see if we can dissect that a bit. I tried to think about stand-alone products in each of those five steps, and produced what may appear a facetious list in table 5.2. But from a stand-alone product point of view, we still generate a lot of information, particularly graphic information, with paper and pencils and pens. We process it the same way, communicate it in the mail, store it in a file drawer, and we reproduce it on a light/lens copier. I see steady evolutionary improvements, but not real revolution in a technology sense.

The trend that we do see more and more is basically toward integrated systems. In these the images or graphics must be converted to bits of information to be processed. I say bits of information as opposed to individual characters.

GENERATION AND REVISION

Let us take the first one, the generation of the data. Currently in the office, the visual display systems and the word processing systems are growing. Simultaneously, they are centralized in processing centers and available at decentralized work areas. More and more memory and computer power is being put into these products right at the work station.

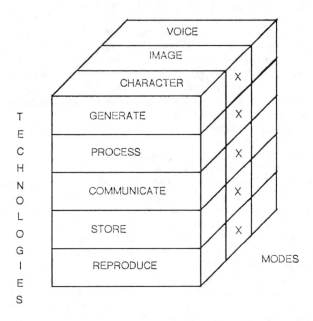

Fig. 5.1. Information technologies and modes.

Table 5.2. For Stand-Alone Products

GENERATE	=	PAPER/PENCIL/PEN
PROCESS	=	ERASERS/PENCIL/PEN
COMMUNICATE	=	MAIL
STORE	=	FILE DRAWER
REPRODUCE	=	LIGHT/LENS COPIER

These products deal with what I call orthographic information, or electronic key stroke character capture. We think they will need to change because they are unable, at present, to process the graphic information. They are able to process only the typewritten word. We see them expanding inward to tie into the data processing system in a company. (This is already happening.) And expanding outward, so that instead of having all of the computing power at one station, we will see decentralized and cheaper stations tying in to the central processor. Another development is a graphics input, and that is really what I want to focus on. Whereas most of the word processors of today have a capability for putting in key stroke data, two technological changes are coming which will add capabilities for graphic input and also for speech. We view these as special systems applications in the photo composition area and in the area of certain things that need to be merged with the text.

With regard to graphics as a special systems application in the area of generation, in the office at least, there are scanners that augment the actual word processors. These are of two kinds: the solid state CCD scanners and the laser scanners. With the CCD scanner one augments the word processing equipment, so that one can scan in graphical data on a piece of paper, display it on the screen and then move it around and change it. These devices generate graphic bits of information, and enable one to arrange, shape, massage, or manipulate that information as one wishes. These, I feel, will play an important role as they coexist with typewriters equipped with optical character readers and voice encoders.

Filing and Retrieval

Assuming we have the bits generated at a work station, either by writing with a pencil and paper or scanning onto a screen, what are some of the things we can do with those bits, and where will they go?

I would like to get some terminology straight. We are talking about a bit as a data element in memory (see table 5.3). We talk about a character such as A, B, C, D. A character can be made from 5 to 7 to 9 or more bits, depending on the quality of the characters you like. One bit per picture element is a black monotone. If you want to get a gray scale, we talk about three bits per picture element and can get up to eight different levels of gray, from light to dark. When we want color, we need 9 to 12 bits per picture element.

Another term used is the resolution or the quality of the picture, whether on a screen or on a piece of paper. Low resolution requires about a hundred by a hundred picture elements per inch. Keep in mind here that we are talking about picture elements per inch, and I said it would be 7 to 9 bits per picture element. Up to 1,000 x 1,000 elements per inch generally gives a very high quality picture. The point I wish to make here is that, once you get into graphics in the office or in office processing, you generate a lot of bits that have to be handled. And the questions are: where is the technology to do that?; what does it cost?; and when is it going to come down so you can start some of these things in the office? Right now we do not have commercial graphic information products in the office environment as part of the workforce. So one of the key areas we are examining, and lots of people are examining, is the storage problem. As we produce all these graphic bits, we will have to have ways to store them. There are many possibilities. I highlight a few in table 5.4.

Table 5.3 Bit Terminology

- 1 BIT = 1 DATA ELEMENT IN MEMORY

- CHARACTERS = 5 X 7 OR 7 X 9 BITS

- PICTURE ELEMENTS = PIXELS OR PEL

- 1 BIT/PEL FOR MONOCHROME
3 BITS/PEL FOR GRAY SCALE - 8 LEVELS
9-12 BITS/PEL FOR COLOR

- RESOLUTION:

    LOW: 100 X 100 PELS

    MEDIUM: 500 X 500 PELS

    HIGH: 1000 X 1000 PELS

Table 5.4 Bits "Stored" in Magnetic Media

- EVOLUTION APPROACHING AREAL DENSITY LIMIT

- THIN FILM MEDIA LATEST INNOVATION

- "REVOLUTIONARY" TECHNOLOGIES:

    - BUBBLES

    - OPTICAL

Just go back in history a little. Look at the history of the rotating memory business. What I have plotted in figure 5.2 is capacity in megabits for the years 1960, 1970 and 1980, starting with the first floating head. The floppy disc, which is still magnetic media, did not come into place until the late 1960s but, as you can see from this schema, magnetic recording technology at that point is starting to approach a limit. It really starts to level off at 10 to the 6th to 10 to the 7th bits per square inch. And at this level we are dealing with recently introduced technology, thin film heads and thin film media. The problem is that as we generate a lot of bits in the office, we are simply running out of capacity on discs to store them.

Another way to look at the memory business is the price per bit, (see figure 5.3) and the access time required for a rotating memory to get the information on and off the disc. In cost terms, we are talking 10 to the -1, or 1/10 of a cent; in access time of 10 to the -2 or .02 seconds. This is a general plot of the technologies; tapes, of course, take longer access time, but are cheaper. What is happening here is that the semiconductor elements are getting cheaper and cheaper, as we all know.   And the two favorite candidates, CCD's or charged couple devices and bubble technology solid state memory chips, are starting to become sufficiently inexpensive to have an impact on the rotating memory disc business.

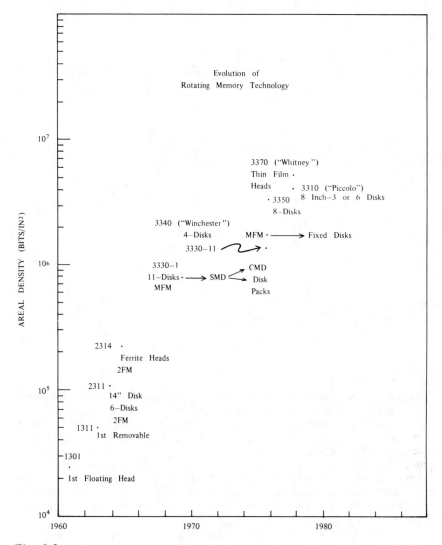

Fig. 5.2

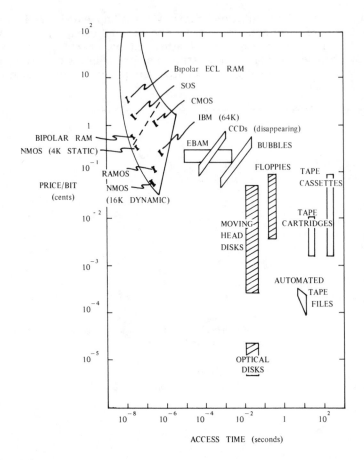

Fig. 5.3.

On the other hand, we have a new technology, extremely inexpensive, called optical disc or optical technology, in which a laser burns a hole in a coated surface. It is archival storage: you can write it once and read it, but you cannot write and then actually erase it. Since this new technology allows lots of bits to be stored, many companies are going into the optical disc business. The reason is simple: the storage media cost is extremely low, lower than any technology we know. On the other hand, bubble technology, nice solid state compact bubble technology, is able to fit right into office equipment, telephones, typewriters, etc.

So the typical questions then arise. How much is it going to cost? When is it going to happen? Lots of people have lots of curves on this and we have our own (see figure 5.4). We are plotting cost and the new technology here in millicents per bit, and you can see that we are getting down to very small numbers. These are the typical MosRam and mini-floppy curves plotted here for 1976-86. We generally try to predict a ten-year span. The semiconductor curves are all pretty much on a downward slope, a decrease of costs by 20 to 30 percent per year for the same kind of function. Bubbles being a new technology they will, we think, be on a much steeper curve until they begin to stabilize and follow the other semi-conductor curves. There is a lot of technological innovation here. We foresee bubbles in '82-'83 making a serious impact on the mini-floppy business, and in the word processing stations and small personal computers that use mini-floppies. On the other hand, we see the optical technology coming into the market in the early '80s and costing well down in the range, almost off the scale.

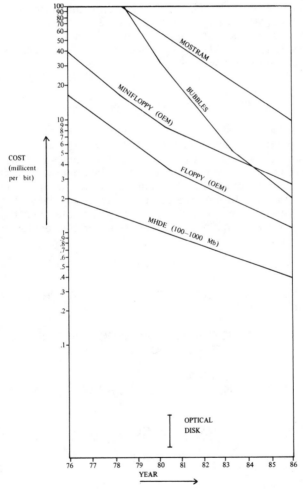

Fig. 5.4.

We will start to see in the early '80s the capability of storing a large number of bits in the office, and that is going to change a lot of things. What is going to happen is that it will be possible to interlink departmental and company files. We will have a real software problem, and it will probably be our biggest problem. How will we keep track of the software codes? Where do all the bits go? How to handle the problems of archival files? When the technologists were first working on optical discs, many people foresaw a problem because once you write something you can't erase it. They predicted that this technology would never replace magnetic systems, unless a rewrite system was devised. Now we are finding out that since we could not solve the rewrite system – it will take another few years – there are some problems. But we have achieved excellent archival systems and there is a lot of use for such archival data, in the legal documents, museum records, etc. Archival storage, achieved by burning a hole in a disc with a laser, enables one to read the data again and to be certain that the data is there and that it is incapable of being erased. This will open up a whole new look at the market place.

Distribution and Communications

Now we have the bits stored, and assuming that we have the memory capacity, the next problem is, can you send them anyplace?

There are trends in this area, with talk of satellites, packet switching networks, among the newer technologies. But from our perspective, communications is the weak link in the whole process right now. This problem will be overcome in the early '80s, but now it takes four to six minutes to send graphic scanned data from the Eastern United States to California with a little stylus writing equipment called facsimile (see table 5.5).

Table 5.5

COMMUNICATIONS - WEAK LINK IN PRESENT GRAPHICS ELECTRONIC SYSTEMS:

FACSIMILE: 4-6 MINUTES NOW IN ANALOG SYSTEMS
             1 MINUTE DIGITAL SOON

- TELEPHONE LINE LIMITATION
- TECHNOLOGY TRENDS ENABLE BROADBAND COMMUNICATIONS:

  - MULTIPLE COPY/MINUTE DOCUMENT DISTRIBUTION VIA:
    - OPTICAL FIBERS
    - CO-AXIAL CABLE ETHERNETS
    - SATELLITES
    - PACKET NETWORKS

There are, however, new compression schemes, new modes of digitizing the data and then sending them over telephone lines. These new digital products are becoming available in the early 1980's, and will enable us to talk of transmission in terms of minutes and sub-minutes. But when you come right down to it, the capacity of that telephone line is the basic problem. Many scientists are at work trying to change that. There are experimental systems that produce multiple copies per minute, so that you can get, say, 60 copies in a minute from New York to California.

There is some resistance to these new experimental systems on the part of recipients who have found present facsimile-sent copies hard to read. If you tell such a user that you are going to send a sixty-page report, you may receive a prayerful request to please mail it. With the mail, we know that the sixty-page report will be a good, legible, hard copy.

This situation is changing rapidly, however. We have at our Palo Alto, California research facility a lot of new experimental equipment. We took out the typewriters and put in fancy word processing stations, interconnected them to an ethernet, which is like a coaxial cable, running all over the building. We took out all the copiers in the building, installed memory banks, and then put in non-impact laser printers that can reproduce the information with excellent quality. We were going to test the paperless society in the office. After a year we went back to measure what was happening. We were generating more paper than ever before. It was so easy to sit at your terminal and say, "I'll take twenty copies." And with the electronic mailbox we have on the screen – something like a telephone book – with everybody's name on it, you can decide who will get copies of this memo you're so proud of, and just check them all off. The electronic printer generates the copy and informs the person to pick up the memo downstairs. The electronic printer is churning away down there, printing more paper than we ever used before, when we had only stand-alone typewriters and copiers.

That is what we call an ethernet, or an internal campus-type network, and it is the trend in the new buildings (see table 5.6). These high speed broad band communications and document distribution networks are feasible within a "campus" structure. The concept is expected to really take off in the manufacturing areas, especially in some of the automobile companies. These companies which produce engines, components, and other products in widely dispersed locations, depend on the various locations keeping abreast through hard copies of changes and specifications in engineering drawings. This we see as a major driving force for adoption. However, the ethernet must be linked to external networks to be really effective in solving the problem.

We foresee a combination of the ethernet and point-to-point networks. We have what we call XTEN, AT&T has the ACS system, and Satellite Business Systems has their own version. With all this activity, I think we will have mega-bit channel communication systems, either from the office or individual workplaces, up to a rooftop transmitter or a telephone line. Certainly, the communications bind in which we are right now, wherein it takes so much time to move graphical data, will disappear in the mid-80s.

Table 5.6.

TREND:

HIGH SPEED DIGITAL BROADBAND COMMUNICATIONS AVAILABLE FROM COMMON CARRIERS

NEXT GENERATION:

DOCUMENT DISTRIBUTION NETWORKS

PROLIFERATION OF INFORMATION SERVICES

CAMPUS NETWORKS – ETHERNET

POINT-TO-POINT NETWORKS: XTEN

Printing and Reproduction

So now we come to the final steps of printing and reproduction, and here there are changes, also. We can do it on soft display, and in this area I see evolutionary changes and not many revolutionary changes. On the other hand, in hard copy generation, I foresee major changes. Let us take a look at these. In the soft display area we go back to World War II and radar, and to the Massachusetts Institute of Technology in the 1950s when soft display started. For some time costs limited the market, and it wasn't until the 1960s that the hardware was really successful. In that, of course, television helped. From our perspective we classify the cathode ray tube or CRT as a mature technology.

We, along with everyone else, have looked at many other kinds of technologies, among them liquid crystal, photochromic plasma, scan converters. All had products associated with them. But none of these technologies really made it to the market place, with the exception of the direct storage tube, first done with M.I.T. and Techtronics.

At present, when we look at soft displays, we see three technologies that dominate: rasterscan, direct beam refresh, and direct view storage tube. Everybody hopes for a flat panel display and there is a good deal of work being done on that. But we don't see it coming before the middle of the 1980s. So we expect the CRT to be around in many different applications for a number of years.

And we see soft display remaining important in new applications. Because all the editing/revision steps going on need some kind of a tube, we expect the cost to continue to decrease. We also expect revolutionary improvements in the technology in terms of clarity of the screen, resolution, etc.

Hard Copy – Computer Graphics

It is in the hard copy area that we see significant changes. Let's just take a look at that. I have tried to put on one figure the whole electronic printing world (see figure 5.5). The chart plots printing from a basic ten characters per second, up to 10,000 lines per minute. The machines for this capacity are out in the field.

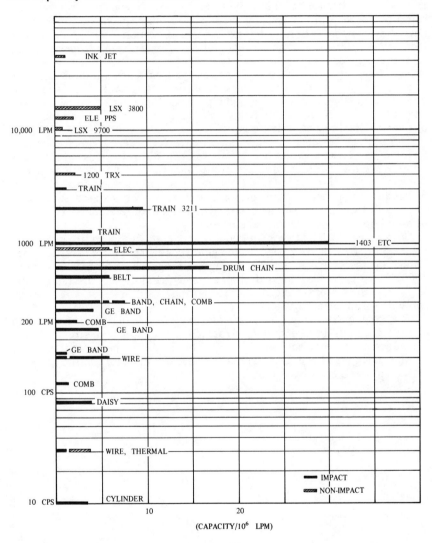

Fig. 5.5. Technical character of industry today. The electronic printing world.

At the middle of the chart, at 1,000 lines per minute, stand the old mechanical workhorses 1401 and 1403, pumping out computer data. Down around   100 characters per second, the technology is mostly mechanical, from a daisy wheel, which we have on our word processors and typewriters, to a comb moving across paper, bands, chains, drives, belts.

When you start to get above a thousand lines per minute, you find that is about as fast as mechanical systems can do things. If you have seen some of those printers working at close to that speed, you marvel at how they can do it.   It is an exacting and complicated process. The industry doesn't think that mechanical devices are going to print faster than that speed.

At the top of the chart you find laser xerography, which is a copier with a laser input that writes bits of information on a drum and then goes through the normal xerographic process of toning which puts marks on paper. These printers handle a whole page at a time. At the high end of over 10,000 lines per minute is the Xerox 9700 and IBM's 3800, working at 20" and 30" per second. The slowest rate for a xerographic engine is about 2" per second, which translates to around a few thousand lines per minute. At this rate, the fastest of the mechanical technologies which are big, huge printers, meet the slowest xerographic device, which can be small, compact, non-impact, and noiseless. We expect such non-impact devices to move into the mainstream of the market as they become more reliable and inexpensive.

In relation to adoption of technology, one always looks at prices (see figure 5.6). This figure reflects the same speed, from ten characters per second up to 10,000 lines per minute, and ranges from $100,000 down to $500. There is a wide range of choices, and technologists are continuing to work on systems like laser xerography and ink jet to improve reliability and lower cost and noise.

We anticipate rapid changes which will bring high speed and high quality graphics to the office. Graphics are coming on strong in the office environment (see figure 5.7). The need is there, the price is coming down, and we can expect significant changes in the present office environment in the 1980s.

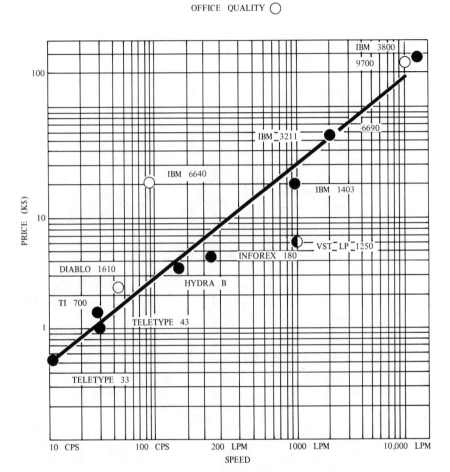

OFFICE   QUALITY ○

Fig. 5.6. Technical character of industry today – price vs. speed.

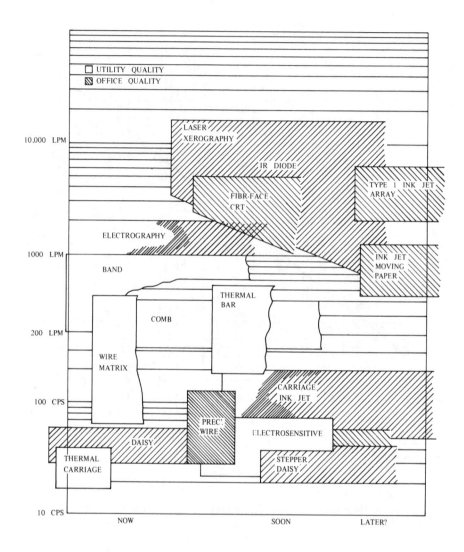

Fig. 5.7. Technology trends. Rapid developments will bring both high speed and high quality graphics to the office.

6 Future Household Communications-Information Systems

E. Bryan Carne

The real-time, electronic communications media (radio, television, and telephone) have had a profound effect on how we live. The modern household depends on them for entertainment, information, social contacts, and assistance. Radio, a broadcast medium, is available virtually everywhere at any time, providing entertainment and information which can be listened to attentively, but which is more often used for background and to provide company. In contrast, television will not stay in the background. It captures the visual sense with a changing image, and demands attention — that is, until the telephone rings, signalling a request for person-to-person communication over any distance.

Now, burgeoning technology makes other media and services possible which may still further affect our life styles. Concepts exist for revolutionary new household communications-information systems, and limited trials have already been made. This chapter briefly speculates on some of the needs which may shape future systems. It notes current demonstrations and trials of advanced communications-information systems around the world, describes three specialized terminals now being tested in the laboratory, and reviews anticipated technical progress which may facilitate future developments. Finally, it presents a concept of a total system, and suggests some restrictions on how products for home communication-information systems may develop.

NEEDS

Advanced technology to support additional communications-information services in the home will be stimulated by consumer demand and provider reward. Both must be present before commercial viability can be assured. What are these needs?

We can speculate. Certainly, some or all of the following are important. For the consumer, the system should be perceived as improving quality of life in some tangible way, such as saving time or money and/or providing fresh opportunities for entertainment and education, or in an intangible way, such as enhancing self-respect, raising mutual esteem, or simply helping to overcome ennui. For selling goods and services, the system should facilitate communications and transactions with the consumer and provide an interface which is amenable to automation (electronic funds transfer, meter reading, etc.). For government (local, state, and federal), the system should facilitate the provision of information or assistance, be equally available to all citizens, and contribute to the common good (by encouraging conservation, for example). And, in general, for industry, academic and service organizations, and government, the system should increase the use of existing products and services, support enhancements, and provide opportunities for new profit (or, in non-profit operations, for entirely new forms of service).

Technological advances, however, are insufficient to ensure the establishment of new communication services. There remains the effect of regulation as practiced by federal, state, and local authorities. Since some of the potential services make use of combinations of communications media, and others combine communications and data processing, the resolution of the many issues they raise will require compromise and patience. Nevertheless, given the potential of commercial viability, such barriers will no doubt eventually be overcome.

ADVANCED COMMUNICATION SYSTEMS AROUND THE WORLD

Demonstrations and field trials of embryo household communications and information systems are under way in other countries. In Japan, some 150 households at Higashi-Ikoma are connected to a model information distribution system. Implemented with two optical fibers per subscriber, which transmit extremely large numbers of signals via light beams, the service provides individual access to video information (static and dynamic) as well as video entertainment and local interest programs. Householder response is accomplished by voice, data, or video messages. Operations began in 1978.

In the same year, residents of some thirty households in suburban Toronto, Ontario, began participation in a field trial in which basic telephone and some video services are provided over single fibers. And in Elie, Manitoba, other households are participating in a field trial which provides a combination of communications capabilities supporting voice, data, and video services, including an advanced information retrieval system.

Since the early 1970s, when work began in earnest in Great Britain, household information retrieval systems have received attention in many countries. Using modified television receivers, the British system displays information carried over a telephone line, or contained in unused lines in the blanking period of a broadcast television signal. In the broadcast mode, the service can be likened to an electronic magazine of a broad size range (100 to 1,000 pages) whose pages are transmitted sequentially and continuously. Special circuits added to the receiver seize, store, and process the data relating to the specific page of information requested by the subscriber. When used with information received over a telephone line, the service can be likened to an electronic encyclopedia with an almost unlimited number of pages. Systems with 250,000 or more pages are practical today and can be stored in a modest computer-controlled data bank.

Whether it be sent over the wires or through the air, CEEFAX, ORACLE and PRESTEL(1) information is transmitted asynchronously (i.e., character by character) in a special code, designated in "8-bit ASCII" which is decoded into "5 x 7 dot matrix elements" and displayed in color in 24 lines of 40 characters each. In the broadcast systems, 6.9M bits/second data are inserted on two lines per field. For a 100-page magazine, because the sequence of pages is transmitted continuously, it may take up to 20 seconds after a request is made for a page to appear. In the wired system, data are sent to the subscriber at 1200 bits/second. Requests from the subscriber are sent at 75 bits/second. A page of information can be called up in a few seconds. In both systems a keypad is used by the subscriber to select the page of information required.

As of the end of 1979, it is estimated that 250,000 British television sets were modified to receive CEEFAX and ORACLE to obtain news, weather forecasts, consumer information, sports results, stock and commodity reports, current events calendars, road conditions reports, etc. In addition, by the time this statement appears, some 20,000 subscribers are expected to be using PRESTEL with an information bank approaching 250,000 pages.

Similar services are being developed in other countries. In France, teletext systems called ANTIOPE and TICTAC are under trial. Using the teletext format of 24 lines of 40 characters each, they offer more flexibility in character formation and transmission speed than the British systems. In one trial, a limited number of pages of weather information were broadcast over a public television channel; in another trial, financial information on stocks and commodities is provided. In Japan, a teletext system called CAPTAINS at this writing is under evaluation. The system uses a central character generator to accommodate ideographic characters.

In Canada, two wired teletext systems are under trial: VISTA provides pages of 20 lines of 32 characters. For graphics, 60 lines of 64 elements can be used. TELIDON incorporates a complex coding scheme which makes it possible to display photographic-like images as well as standard graphics and alpha-numerics. Other improvements relate to economy of transmission and use with variable resolution terminals. Telidon may be characterized as a second-generation information retrieval system. Several other countries, including the Federal Republic of Germany, Holland, Sweden, Finland, Switzerland, and Hong Kong, are planning or testing national teletext services.

In summary, there exist in the world today several pockets of activity directed towards implementing advanced communications and information services for the householder. As yet, none of the trials has established beyond a reasonable doubt that there is a legitimate need for such services. More options and opportunities must be explored in order to test the full gamut of potential offerings and point the way to those for which there may be a sustained public demand and a reasonable expectation of commercial viability.

THE SITUATION IN THE UNITED STATES

Today, in the United States, nearly every household is connected to an electric utility, and is equipped with at least a radio, a television, and a telephone. Almost one in five of all TV households is connected to a cable which distributes several channels of television. A few cable households have a degree of return communications – primarily alarms, or low-data rate response services which allow the viewer to talk back to questions or comments, engage in surveys, or play games. Approximately one in twenty cable households subscribes to a form of pay-TV, and a small number of TV households receive broadcast pay-TV. The feasibility of communicating with electricity-users by radio, telephone line, television cable, or over the power line to read meters or effect load control, has been demonstrated.

With government assistance, several experimental, two-way CATV (cable TV) installations have been implemented for limited periods to demonstrate the feasibility of providing social services by cable. In general, they have been judged successful, although few have survived the termination of federal funds. A wideband switched cable information system using "frame grabbers" (i.e., transmitting a whole frame of information at a time) has been developed. The cost, however, is generally considered to be prohibitive in the foreseeable future. Other cable TV information systems are available which distribute information as analog television frames.

Until recently, little commercial interest in teletext systems was evident. Now, however, a national television network is evaluating both French and British broadcast teletext systems. An affiliated station is transmitting teletext on lines 15 and 16 of the television signal to produce a page comprising 20 lines of 32 characters. A supplier to the cable TV industry has developed a teletext system that will allow cable operators to supply alphanumeric information to subscribers. A multi-point television distribution company has developed a broadcast tele-text system in which 3.8M bits/second data (i.e., roughly 600 words per second) are inserted on two lines in the television signal to produce a page comprising 20 lines by 40 characters. Plans for national distribution to cable operators by satellite have been announced.

Some 200 farmers in Kentucky are beginning to receive weather-crop-related information over modified government-supported wired teletext system known as Green Thumb. A major publishing corporation has announced a two-year pilot project to test interest in wired teletext. Weather, news, sports results, movie schedules, etc. will be made available to 150 to 200 homes. A major telecommunications corporation has recently been licensed to offer VIEWDATA/PRESTEL service in the United States. A market trial is planned after modification of the software to run on a United States computer, with identification of information providers.

In summary, although the United States has more communications equipment per capita than any other country in the world, the development of advanced communications and information systems lags behind other countries. I attribute this in part to an uncertain regulatory environment, in part to the absence of a tradition of central standardization, and in part to the very nature of private enterprise.

SOME EXPERIMENTAL SERVICES

While information retrieval could become an important household function, it is not the only capability that advanced technology can provide. Other, more complex chores can be performed by specialized terminals that combine microprocessors with relatively conventional hardware to perform communications — information tasks dictated by user motivations of conservation, entertainment, or personal security. The general features and intent of such equipment can be illustrated by describing three experimental units now in the laboratory. They are based on a residential load center, a television receiver, and a telephone.

Load Control and Energy Management

When excess demand for electricity occurs because of severe weather, or other circumstances, utilities have no option but to shed load in order to maintain system stability. For the householder, this generally means a period of intermittent or total blackout By providing means to shave these peaks, it will be possible to reduce the frequency of such occurrences, conserve fuel, and reduce the need for expensive, inefficient peak-load generating equipment. At present, voluntary compliance, time-of-day pricing, and automatic load control are being evaluated to achieve these goals. Of these techniques, the last is of interest here.

The elements of a load control and energy management system are shown in figure 6.1. In the load center the primary power circuit is divided into individual circuits connected to loads comprising lights, appliances, etc. These connections are controlled by commands from the utility and/or the householder. Major loads, such as water heater, space heater, air conditioner, etc., may be turned off or on by the utility using a command carried by radio, telephone line, cable TV, or the power line. These and other loads can also be controlled by the householder him- or herself, using an adaptive device set to prevent the total load from exceeding some limit, by manual controls.

The system may also include a display. In its simplest form, this might be a signal lamp which is illuminated on command from the utility to signify that cycling of the major loads has begun and that all but essential loads should be shed, or that a blackout is imminent. The display might also include a household meter to provide information on current load. More sophisticated units could give historical information and perform limited analysis of recent consumption. In areas where time-of-day pricing is employed, time would be an important input both to the householder's programmer and to his display.

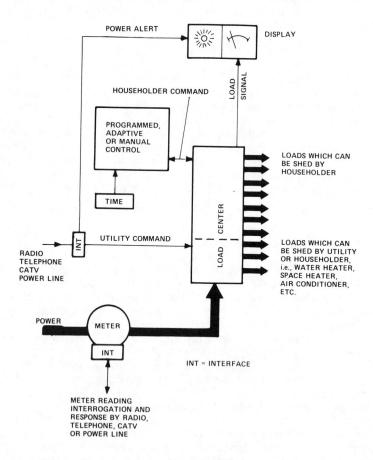

Fig. 6.1. Load Control and Energy Management, illustrating the use of a "smart" load center. It receives commands from the utility or the householder to manage the load presented by household activities so as to contain peak demand or minimize cost.

Programmable Entertainment/Information Center

In a television receiver, the introduction of microprocessor-based control and electronic actuation allows the selection of channels in random order and makes other features possible. For instance, the receiver can be programmed to provide automatic reception of specific channels at specific times for viewing or recording; a sequence of instructions can be entered to ensure that interesting programs are not missed: day, date, time, and channel number can be superimposed on the picture at will, etc. What is more, simple messages can be composed, stored, retrieved, and displayed as a means of family communication. If a teletext service is available, signal decoding, page selection, and storage of additional information can be accomplished. Graphics can be generated by local input to the microprocessor, and, with the addition of light pencils or other suitable input devices, games can be played.

Figure 6.2 shows the basic elements of a programmable entertainment and information center. The degree of flexibility that can be achieved is largely dependent on the capability of the microprocessor (Central Processing Unit [CPU] and Memory) at the bottom of the diagram. With the exception of Teletext, which is already formatted and flows through the decoder to the display generator and thence to the video amplifiers in the receiver, all other functions and displays can be constructed from, and controlled by, information (programs and data) placed in memory (RAM, random-access memory and/or ROM, pre-wired "read only" memory that cannot be changed by the user).

For time-dependent control of the receiver functions, a programmable, non-volatile memory is required to store the channel selections programmed by the viewer for automatic activation, and to keep track of the channel to which the receiver is tuned (in order to protect this information in the event of power loss). If desired, an audible alarm can be included to alert the viewer that the automatic feature has been invoked and the receiver has been turned on. Silencing the alarm confirms the action. If this is not done within a pre-set time, the receiver turns off automatically. In one embodiment of such a system, approximately 4,000 bytes of memory (i.e., groups of bits operated upon as a unit) are used to list pre-programmed channels (including viewer edit and prompt routines), provide automatic activation, and display day, date, time, and channel number on demand.

For playing games and similar functions, more memory is needed. By using sophisticated coding, and limiting the complexity of the presentation, a color picture can be described in approximately 200 bytes. Movement of the entire picture in a "wrap around mode" can be achieved by scanning a larger memory; and fast, smooth, complex motion can be had by the use of additional "foreground" memory, or specifically pre-empted ("dedicated") symbol of hardware. The detection of symbol-to-symbol and symbol-to-background collisions (required in many games) can be performed in hardware which may also contain rules for determining which symbol shall dominate. New game programs can be loaded from a cassette or by the substitution of a different ROM module. Many such games are commercially available and will become continually more sophisticated.

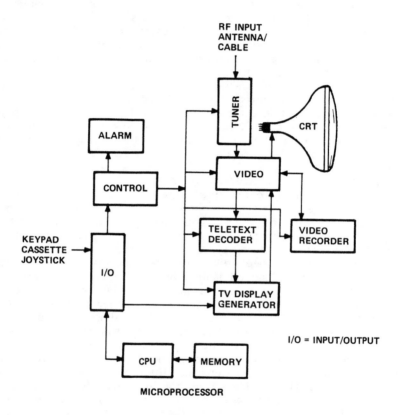

Fig. 6.2. Programmable Entertainment and Information Center. By adding a microprocessor, input devices, control logic, and a display generator, a conventional television receiver, capable of being turned on and off at times determined by the householder, can be used to play games and display information.

Remote Control and Monitor Telephone

The average household telephone circuit is used as a talking path a very small fraction of the day, perhaps only as much as 30 minutes. Furthermore, it is useless as a voice communications medium unless someone is present to answer it. However, by providing additional electronics, the telephone line can be used for new services such as meter reading, alarm reporting, and remote control and monitoring of household facilities. Such a system is sketched in figure 6.3. It comprises an input-output interface block; a microprocessor; a main telephone, with extensions, if desired; a display panel for circuit testing, status reporting and insertion of data; a message recorder; and connections to devices to be controlled and/or monitored.

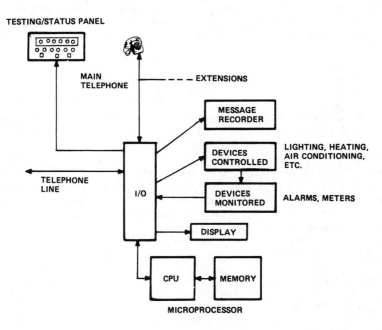

Fig. 6.3. Remote Control and Monitor Telephone. Adding a micro-processor and other devices to a conventional telephone will allow equipment to be monitored and controlled remotely, emergency services to be summoned automatically, and selected information to be displayed as desired.

To control and/or monitor the status of household devices from afar, the householder calls his household telephone. Assuming no one is at home, ringing will proceed until, at a predetermined time after ringing has commenced, automatic circuits place a message recorder on the line which responds with, "one moment, please. . . ." or similar words. This is followed by a pause during which the caller (householder) can transmit a coded signal identifying himself by pressing the push buttons on the originating telephone. (If the telephone set he is using has a rotary dial, he must have an auxiliary device to generate the needed tones that can be accommodated by the telephone system. Such devices are available which attach to the mouthpiece of the handset, or can be held in the hand). If no signal is received in this interval, the message recorder proceeds to tell the caller that the householder is not at home, and gives instructions for leaving a message. If the correct coded signal is received, a short acknowledgement tone is generated. The message recorder is then removed, and the equipment is made ready to receive coded instructions from the householder inquiring as to the status of specific facilities, and directing that household systems be turned on/off. Receipt of each inquiry or command is acknowledged by a distinctive tone or combination of tones. A typical set of inquiries, commands, and responses used in an experimental system is given in Table 6.1.

Table 6.1 Monitoring Household Devices
by Telephone

GENERAL INFORMATION: The telephone will ring for approximately 15 seconds before the controller places an answering device on the line. During these 15 seconds, a person may answer the telephone in the normal manner. Once the answering device is connected, the message "one moment please" is sent. The caller then has five seconds to identify himself (by a touch-tone coded number) or the answering device will proceed to invite the caller to leave a message. If the caller correctly identifies himself, the controller sends a "proceed-to-send" tone and awaits further input.

CALLER COMMAND		DTMF CODE
EQUIPMENT A,	TURN ON	*12
	TURN OFF	*13
EQUIPMENT B,	TURN ON	*14
	TURN OFF	*15

CALLER INQUIRY	DTMF CODE
IS EQUIPMENT A ON?	*16
IS EQUIPMENT B ON?	*17

RESPONSE	TONE
PROCEED-TO-SEND	800 Hz, 1 SECOND
ACKNOWLEDGE	800 Hz, INTERRUPTED, 1/SECOND
BUSY	400 Hz, INTERRUPTED, 1/SECOND
YES	800 Hz, INTERRUPTED, 2/SECONDS
NO	800/400 Hz, ALTERNATING

The input/output circuitry contains a ring detector, a tone detector, an analog/digital converter (which changes the variable intensity form of the incoming signal to the "digital" or pulse form) for decoding in the microprocessor, and an answering tone generator. The microprocessor interprets the received signals, executes the appropriate functions, and sends the appropriate code to the answering tone generator. Besides responding to a call, the system can also place calls in response to signals from alarms, transmitting data messages to appropriate answering points. Operation can be tested by using a status panel or other display. In an advanced experimental unit, a color display is used for presentation of information, including wired teletext and directory assistance.

BURGEONING TECHNOLOGY

The advanced communications developments around the world, and the experimental terminals just described, have been made possible by rapidly developing technology. Future progress will depend largely on continuing advances in three major areas:

1. The attainment of higher levels of integration (i.e., more active elements in the same space) in digital circuits. Today, the most complex integrated circuit in use is a memory containing 64,000 bits. By 1985, expected advances in chip size, element density, circuit design, and other improvements will produce chips containing at least one million elements. The availability of these devices will lead to entire systems on a chip, to more powerful processors, and to the diffusion of machine intelligence to even the smallest equipment. Other storage techniques, such as magnetic "bubbles," will provide non-volatile mass-memories (i.e., memories in which the information is not lost when the power is cut off). These super-chips will be characterized by relatively small size and extremely low cost, giving renewed impetus to implementing more and more features in a digital fashion and producing a continuing demand for low cost, analog/digital and digital/analog conversion, using techniques which can be readily executed in integrated circuit form.

The super-chips will contain a flexible assortment of logic and storage elements which can be configured to suit specific applications. Their operation will be determined by combinations of functions configured in hardware, firmware (a form of fixed programming), and software (programming). Much new equipment for personal and household use will be developed, using these chips as the cost of digital electronics continues to decline.

2. The operation of satellite circuits at higher frequencies. Satellites such as those launched into space in recent years provide a relatively simple way of communicating over long distances, independent of terrestrial obstacles. They also provide a platform from which to broadcast signals over wide areas of the globe. While the orbital slots from which satellites operating at specified, extremely high frequency (4/6 GHz, GHZ being 10^{12} cycles per second) can broadcast signals to North America are virtually filled, space is still available at 11/14 GHz, and the entire orbital arc is available at 18/30 GHz. At these very high frequencies the radiation pattern from the spacecraft can be split into many "spot" beams, each focussing on a small area on the surface of the

earth, thereby allowing the same frequencies to be used in different geographical areas ("frequency re-use"). To their disadvantage, signals at these frequencies are subject to interruption by heavy rainfall. Nevertheless, they offer a relatively unimpeded facility for national distribution of information and entertainment of the kind that would be of great value to the development of communications-information services.

3. The development of a complete range of optical communications products.   Optical fibers provide a wideband transmission path of extremely small physical cross-section free from power and radio frequency interference. Point-to-point communications applications have already been demonstrated, including transmission of digital signals inside the telephone network, and transmission of video signals for video conferencing and cable TV. Longer wavelength, higher power sources, and improved detectors will allow the use of longer spans between repeaters (i.e., between the devices which step up the signal strength at required intervals). Higher-performance fibers will extend this limit even further, providing a trouble-free alternative for the transmission of information and entertainment over the distances typically encountered in urban-suburban environments. Effective local distribution of mixed signals (voice, data, and video) will be possible as soon as adequate networking components have been perfected (thereby encouraging economical duplex operation over a single fiber, and the use of shared distribution facilities), and when some form of optical switch has been developed. The latter could be an important component in the local distribution of any significant amount of personal video services.

While not of equal importance, three other technical areas could strongly influence the development of household communications and information systems. One is the development of natural language (i.e., close to English) programming for microprocessors so the householder can redirect his or her equipment at will. The second is the development of low-cost alternatives to the color picture tube, both larger sizes (picture-on-the wall) and smaller sizes (personal displays). The third is the development of small, robust, high-performance, color video cameras.

A Total Concept

Stimulated by this combination of new technologies, an all-encompassing household communications-information system is conceivable, as shown in figure 6.4. The system is centered on a home computer which supports three subsystems: information and entertainment, command and control, and administration. It receives radio signals transmitted over the air, television signals broadcast both from terrestrial and satellite facilities and from cable, administrative signals from the electric utility over the air, over the power lines, or over the telephone or cable, and signals from the telephone network. A myriad of household products and appliances can be controlled by, provide input to, or interact with, the system. In principle, a single wideband connection (optical fiber) could serve to link the system to the world.

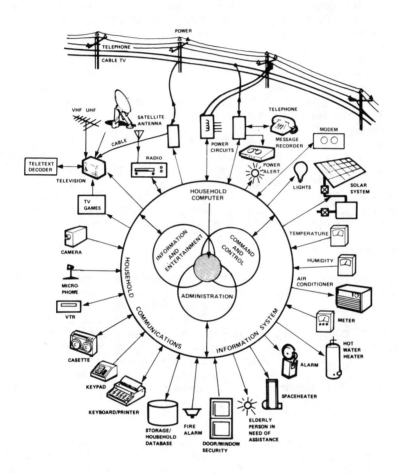

Fig. 6.4. A Total Household Communications-Information System. A conceptualization of a household system in which communications are provided by power line, telephone, cable TV, and broadcast services, and household activities are performed by sub-systems supported by a household computer.

Briefly, besides the familiar uses of the radio, television, and telephone, some of the additional functions which each sub-system could perform are:

Information and Entertainment

Provide retrieval of catalog, schedule and library information, news, reports, etc., using equipment such as a television receiver, teletext decoder, telephone, modem (telephone line interface), keypad, or keyboard/printer. These would be supported by broadcast teletext services, wired teletext services, community services, or other information sources.

Provide interactive education for pre-school, in-school, vocational and continuing students, and interested adults, using equipment such as a television receiver, video and/or audio recorder, microphone, television camera, and keypad or keyboard/printer. These would be supported by pre-recorded material or community services.

Provide interactive games and intellectual entertainment for children and adults, using equipment such as a television receiver, television games attachment, video and/or audio recorder, keypad or keyboard/printer. These would be supported by pre-recorded material, community services, or other subscribers.

Provide interactive entertainment, opinion polling, preference sampling, possibly even voting, using equipment such as television receiver and keypad, supported by broadcast and cable services.

Command and Control

Adjust electrical load by time-of-day or remote command from utility. Provide meter information to utility on-demand, or at pre-set intervals. Optimize use of solar panels, air conditioning, space heaters, etc. to maintain living environment within pre-set temperature and humidity limits, yet conserve energy consumption. Monitor fire, intrusion, and assistance alarms, notifying emergency services or community center as appropriate. Provide system status information to remote caller (householder). Turn on lights, radio, heat, etc. on command (local or remote) or in accordance with a pre-set scenario.

Administration

Provide interactive information retrieval using equipment such as television receiver, video, and/or audio-recorder, household data base, keypad or keyboard/printer. These would be supported by pre-recorded material, remote data centers, or community services. Maintain family records such as accounts, medical history, addresses, telephone numbers, etc. Pay bills by electronic funding transfers. Compute taxes. Send messages to, and receive messages from other subscribers (electronic mail).

The above listings are by no means exhaustive. Indeed, many more items of household equipment (such as washer, dryer, oven, freezer, water and gas meters, etc.) could be added, and many more specialized features included. Suffice it to say that a computer and ancillary equipment can automate almost all household functions requiring intellectual (as opposed to physical) activity, and they can pass beyond the individual household when supported by appropriate local data banks and community services, or even nationwide services (perhaps distributed by satellite). To implement the full package with today's technology would at this time be enormously expensive, but possible. Future technology will make the task easier, and if every household were to be so equipped, economies gained from volume production could well make the cost affordable.

IMPLICATIONS

The ideas embodied in figure 6.4 illustrate the potential of advanced technologies to provide additional communications-information services which might be attractive to consumers and providers. Such unifying models can be helpful to the working technologist. However, it would be a mistake to attribute a reality beyond this and assume that a total system of this sort must emerge. To do so would be to ignore the influence of existing interests and the importance of existing facilities.

The present communications providers and the industries that support them will greatly influence the course developments will take. Many of these organizations see opportunities to extend their present markets, thereby creating not one all-embracing communication-information system, but many partial systems, exploiting the base provided by existing products. In addition, the idea of one system providing many diverse services flies in the face of the present fragmentation of communications providers and public utilities. These too, will lend strong support to the development of more specialized systems.

The three experimental terminals show what added capability a microprocessor can bring to existing facilities to turn them into relatively sophisticated household communications-information terminals. Such systems would provide services that could have significant appeal in the future when the cost has been reduced and a supporting provider infrastructure has been developed. Each is a nucleus around which the three sub-systems of figure 6.4 could develop. They appear to fulfill many of the needs listed earlier.

Who can tell what additional capability will be added if broadcasting satellites and optical fibers become commonplace? Certainly, the headlong rush of technical developments will be adequate to support any innovative services the householder may require. What will happen depends on 1) how much sophisticated equipment society is willing to endure (or can afford) to achieve conservation, fulfillment, and security; and 2) whether the many non-technological obstacles posed by government regulation and private interests, at all levels, can be overcome.

NOTES

(1) A certain amount of confusion has arisen over nomenclature. The original descriptions of the British systems referred to "broadcast and wired Teletext systems." Specific services provided by the television authorities and the telephone administration are CEEFAX and ORACLE (broadcast teletext) and PRESTEL (wired teletext). Until recently, PRESTEL was named VIEWDATA, and Viewdata has been used by many to denote this general class of information retrieval systems. Now, some authorities are recommending that the term Teletext be used to denote broadcast teletext, and Videotex be used to denote wired teletext.

(2) Portions of the text for this chapter have been republished from the article entitled "The Wired Household," appearing in IEEE Spectrum, October 1979, pp. 61 to 66, © 1979 IEEE.

7 Worldwide Information Services

Raymond W. Marshall

Much of today's literature on computers and electronics talks about how small things are getting, how we can obtain more computational capacity in a smaller box. We read about minicomputers, microcomputers, microprocessors; and in the world of communications we talk about fiber optics and laser beam technology. While the literature is not quite so dramatic at the upper end of computing and communications, the evolution there is just as dramatic. We now have more powerful computational capacity than we've ever had in a single entity. We can now communicate over longer distances than ever before. And there seems to be no end to this rapid growth.

NEW DEMANDS AND SERVICES

The intersection of communications and computing comprises the new world of the informational services. While technology is pushing things forward, another set of demands is rising, demands from the people who operate the many activities in business enterprises. They are creating demands in corporations to do things differently than they have been done in the past. For example, they're talking about cutting hours, days, and perhaps even weeks off financial consolidations. They're talking about plant "sourcing" on a worldwide basis. It's the combination of the available technology and the demands of business enterprise that are making worldwide information service possible, necessary, and desired.

One such worldwide service is the General Electric MARK III service. (There are other first-class broad-scale information networks in government and in the private sector. It is, however, fair to say that the General Electric network is the largest and has a lengthy history of pushing the state of the art). I'm going to use the MARK III system as the basis for most of my discussion. I will then follow with four examples to illustrate how worldwide information service interrelates with business enterprise.

You might think that the only thing necessary to put a computer information network together is to place a complex in a facility of computers and then connect it with some form of communication such as WATS, which is a wide area telephone service, connected to the computer, and available on an international basis. That is not the case. There are certain elements of service quality that require you to take advantage of technology immediately as you deploy and develop your network. Around-the-clock availability, for example. Rapid response is demanded by stringent business applications. As I describe the basic technologies, you will see how service quality plays its role in deciding the type of network that's best for a given situation. The technology can be described by considering three areas, a) generation, b) transmission, and c) distribution. These are analogous to power generation, power transmission, and power distribution. Generation refers to the center containing processing capacity. Transmission, similar to high voltage transmission, refers to the high band width or long distance data communication paths. Distribution means carrying the information from some distribution centers to the points of consumption which, in the case of an information network, are known as terminals.

The generation centers, large-scale, have been especially prepared for the needs of the modern computer. They are high security installations with independent power systems and the "plumbing" that large-scale modern computers require.

Computers Not Good Enough

Even though today's manufacturing and the design techniques of the modern computer are light years ahead of yesterday's, the present computer is still not good enough for worldwide information service in terms of service quality. Some technique must be employed that can bring service quality close to the 100 percent level needed for information utility grade service.

Let me elaborate. In a standard computer complex there is usually a one-to-one relationship between the processor and the files. The act of computing is to bring a customer's data and program into the memory of the processor and then act upon it by a set of instructions. With today's computer technology, it's not unreasonable to expect that the main frame (the central processor of the computer system) manufactured by IBM, Honeywell, Burroughs, CDC, or other manufacturers to provide a service quality at the 96 to 98 percent level. But if you're going to operate in the service arena you have to have something on the order of 99½ to 100 percent service quality. So you employ some type of technological technique to overcome the inherent lack of such near-perfect quality in the manufactured computer. A technique that we use in the MARK III System is called "clustering of the systems." This is a way of putting groups of computers together in a cluster – there can be up to eight large computers in a cluster – so that any one processor can gain access to the files of any other.

This technique seems simple to describe but it has taken several years of technological innovation to put it into place. For diversity of operation, a worldwide system will have multiple super centers. In the MARK III System we have three centers located in Rockville, Maryland, just north of Washington; in Cleveland, Ohio; and in Amsterdam, Holland. Each of these is conditioned to the highest standards required for information services.

Inside a computer complex you would see the array of computers and file equipment where customers' files are stored. That, in simple terms, is the generation portion of a worldwide information service.

TRANSMISSION

Now let's turn to communication, and look first at the area of transmission.   Once more, service quality places a high demand on technology. It's unreasonable to expect that communications never fail. So some form of technological innovation must be available to nullify the potential failure of communications.   Two or three different techniques are used in concert to overcome long distance communication failures. In our operation, we use what is called a "store and forward" communication system, which is fairly common in the industry. Messages outbound from the processing center to the terminal are stored in communication computers which are adjacent to central processors. They're called central concentrators on this diagram. They communicate with computers called remote concentrators or RC on this diagram. The distance between the two might be thousands of miles. Store and forward communications require outbound messages to be stored in the central concentrator until the remote concentrator acknowledges that it has received the transmission. In the event the remote concentrator does not receive, then the process is repeated until the remote concentrator does receive the transmission.

Inbound messages are processed the same way, moving from the remote concentrator terminal in which they are stored until the central concentrator acknowledges receipt of the transmission.

That technique overcomes short-term outages. But suppose there's a long-term outage of the communication path, and then you're down because the computer can only store so much information. In such a case we employ two circuits between each central concentrator and remote concentrator. They're under software control so either line can carry the full load. In the event of a single outage, the transmission is still sustained. But that does not overcome the common physical event. Suppose that you have both of them on a satellite circuit or both of them on an undersea cable. Then you could have a common outage which would take out the entire circuit. The obvious answer is to employ <u>both</u> satellite circuit and undersea cable for the two lines. If you employ two lines over separate geographical routings, it's rare that you will have a simultaneous outage of both. An undersea cable operates with less time delay than a satellite circuit. To compensate for the time difference, the transmission network connects the processing centers to distribution points, which have to be strategically located around the world. Virtually every form of long-haul communications is utilized — satellite circuits, microwave, undersea cables; and they operate on all band widths, all the way from the voice grade circuit, which operates near three kilobauds up to the high band width circuits at 230 kilobauds. Network control is executed by sophisticated centers located adjacent to the central processors. And since transmission circuits are provided by international common carriers, we maintain close liaison with the international carriers. These are Western Union, IT&T, RCA and their interconnecting domestic AT&T long-haul operators.

I cannot overemphasize the importance of communicating with the international common carriers. This is probably one of the biggest reasons for improved service quality in our long-haul circuits. These individuals have to speak the language — the language of phase shift and phase jitter — and the language that the international carriers understand, so that we can get rapid response to problems. These are some of the practical aspects of the worldwide service.

DISTRIBUTION TECHNOLOGY

Let's turn to distribution technology. This means, simply, getting from the strategically located distribution points to the end user. GE has 21 locations throughout the world serving as distribution points to some 600 cities. We use local and long-haul circuits for the connections. In some of those links we use store-and-forward communications as well. The 21 locations are strategically placed on four continents.

Distribution control is maintained by personnel trained in the local language. This is not the international carrier's language but the local carrier's language, which is a different one altogether. You may think that the carriers in the United States or around the world operate with some common heartbeat. They don't. Even in the United States, the Bell System is not a single system. It's a collection of independent companies. They all operate to their own heartbeat and you have to know how to talk with them. This is complicated overseas as you have to be able to talk with the local communications suppliers who are the Post, Telegraph & Telephone (PT&T) agencies. You have to speak not only <u>their</u> version of the PT&T

language but really their language, be it French or Japanese. So it gets to be quite a problem. If you resolve it, you can put a first-class system into place.

I'd like now to turn to four applications of the information service, to give you a feel of how it relates to the business community. If there is anything that the applications have in common, it is the old proverb, time is money. Business enterprises realize that if they can do things more rapidly, they can improve the bottom line of performance. It's also true that if a corporation can do that, it may win a competitive edge. So there is little reluctance to use worldwide information services.

Keeping Track Worldwide

The first application is the case history of American Express. This company has some nine million credit card holders. It maintains an extensive in-house computer system and a worldwide network. American Express uses a worldwide information service in addition to its own, to provide additional capability. The challenge was to monitor the financial affairs of American Express affiliates in various locations around the world, principally Europe, Mexico, and Australia. The corporation wanted its affiliates producing a common set of financial reports, which would enable a consolidation of activity on one balance sheet. Only in this way could the parent company get an adequate picture of what's really going on around the world. The advantage of a worldwide information service for American Express was, then, to employ an existing network without having to develop the application for itself. The result: American Express feels that budgets and expenses are in control to a degree never before achieved. An additional advantage is the rapidity with which currency conversions can now be made.

Energy Exploration

PSI Energy is a company engaged in making assessments of oil exploration. It is also an author, having developed some sophisticated software packages for·those firms that are doing oil well exploration. By placing the software package on a worldwide information network, PSI can use it as a distribution service to reach their customers. PSI charges a premium, so that every time their program is run they get a premium billing out of its execution, not unlike the royalties an author gets from his books. One of the fastest-growing areas of information service is the use of sophisticated authored software. PSI's software system is called POGO, short for Profitability of Oil and Gas Opportunity. The service evaluates the oil well activity before the exploration process gets to the point of drilling the well. Only one out of ten oil wells is successful. It is obviously desirable to have a total analysis done before drilling is begun. PSI analyzes such things as economic impact, return on investment, cost-benefit. The system also maintains financial data, like cash flow and customer performance. The advantages are: the information gives clear insight as to the advisability of continuing with the drilling before committing too heavy a burden of available resources. And because oil and gas explorations are going on on a worldwide basis, PSI Energy has been able to reach interested parties all over the world, through worldwide communication computing service.

Currency Control

The third application is in the area of currency control. The European/American Bank decided to put a currency data base on a system which would provide updates concerning the current value of currency on a worldwide basis. Software was then developed for some 200 clients, who are counseled as to their financial position on a daily basis, or even hourly if they wish.

In this arena, there is a rapidly emerging data base activity on a worldwide scale.

Export-Import Application

The final application I have chosen is Peugeot and the worldwide manufacturing and distribution points of the Peugeot automobile. Peugeot, as you know, manufactures a relatively high quality automobile in France and markets it worldwide, as most manufacturers do. After manufacture, the car is turned over to one of Peugeot's wholly-owned subsidiaries for transportation. In the United States it is imported by Peugeot, Inc. There was a problem: so many automobiles in the pipeline that Peugeot was getting locked up in export-import paper work. Moreover, the company didn't know precisely what was in the pipeline.

To remedy the situation, Peugeot installed two data bases, one at the point of manufacture, the other at the point of import. In France, the data base was given the characteristics of automobiles released to the transportation carrier. Peugeot, Inc., in the United States built its own data base with information on cars on order. The two data bases were "played" together, and it was then possible to have information about the cars which were being moved for Peugeot, Inc., in the United States, which triggered off the export paper work and the import paper work so the cars would not be held up in transit. Peugeot feels that "float" of automobiles has been considerably reduced.

It is clear, as these four applications demonstrate, that worldwide information services play a vital role in the everyday activities of business enterprise, a role that is going to continue and increase.

8 Office of the Future
Joseph Agresta

What is meant by the "Office of the Future?" To some, this phrase conjures up a vision of a dehumanized "1984" society controlled by machines and perhaps a small elite group of technocrats. To others, the vision resembles a leisure-oriented utopia where everyone works out of his or her own home and deals with the world through a myriad of wondrous electronic devices. The truth is that we cannot really predict what the office of the future will be like. It is almost certain that electronic technology will play a dominant role; it is also certain that the "atmosphere" created will depend on people and how they choose to use the technology.

The view of this chapter is relatively short-range. We discuss current technologies and how they will help evolve a different kind of office within a relatively short period of years. Our approach is that while the end result is revolutionary, the sensible path is evolutionary.

Background

Essentially, two driving forces will lead us to the automated office. Both are related to costs — first, the costs of people, and second, the costs of technology.

In the early 1980s, there seems to be little prospect for major improvement in the inflationary spiral. People costs will continue to rise. Key to reducing the effects of rising personnel costs is increased productivity, i.e., each individual must "produce" more than he or she is currently producing, so that the cost per unit "product" is not increased as the worker's salary increases. During the period of the 1950s through

---

*The ideas collected in this paper result from the work of a number of my past and present colleagues, including G.W. Bond, S.R. Dzubow, R.F. Henshaw, F.J. LoSacco, and D.H. Posmantier.

the 1970s, productivity in manufacturing and agriculture has been significantly improved through the introduction of automation. This has been accomplished through a capital investment in suitable equipment to the extent of $25,000 to $35,000 per worker.

Meanwhile back at the office, little has been done. As workload increases, the normal approach is to increase staff, with the consequent increase in overhead costs. There has been only a modest investment, averaging $2,000 per worker, in equipment, which may be considered comparable to the automated systems introduced in manufacturing and agriculture. It is no surprise that productivity has not improved.

At the same time, new developments in technology have reduced the costs of computer-related equipment. The development of integrated circuits, semiconductor memories, bubble memories, microprocessors, etc. have significantly extended the potential application of computer techniques. Everyone is familiar with the dramatic decrease in price and the increase in capability of small hand-held calculators. Other evidence is the availability and popularity of personal computers. It is now possible to visit your local electronics shop and purchase, at a cost comparable to audio or video entertainment equipment, a computer whose capabilities challenge those of computers which in the 1950s and 1960s cost hundreds of thousands of dollars and could be afforded only by the largest corporations.

This technology has begun to have an impact in the office primarily through display-type word processors and electronic document distribution systems. These will promote the development of electronic filing systems, and will interface with data processing applications and multifunction communication systems. The effective use of these new capabilities will require new designs of organization and new ways of doing work.

Computers have been effectively used to automate transaction-type business systems such as accounting, order processing, and inventory control. In many cases, this was accomplished by a relatively literal translation of manual systems to computer systems. The workers now dealt with input cards and output scrolls instead of ledgers and tub files, but they had not really altered the way of doing work. This has changed somewhat in recent years through the introduction of interactive systems which allow them to work directly with the computer rather than with its products.

This people-computer interface is the most critical area which will determine the effectiveness, and ultimately the cost-benefit bottom line, resulting from office automation. People normally resist change, and often for good reasons. Their instincts will sometimes detect real problems not obvious to the promoter of change. On the other hand, they will readily accept change and new technology when they recognize its value and understand how it will help accomplish their jobs. It is management's main challenge to insure that office technology is introduced in a manner that does provide useful change. People's concerns must be addressed and answered realistically and honestly. Improper attention to the human aspects of the situation can only result in improper application of the technology, and either failure or serious reduction in the achievement of the real benefits available.

Word Processing

Word processing is important for two reasons: first, it is the most advanced manifestation of office automation already in use; and second, it is the building block for a whole host of technologies which together form the essence of the office of the future.

The term "word processing" was invented by IBM in conjunction with new devices such as the Memory Typewriter and the Magnetic Tape Selectric Typewriter (MTST) which incorporated an electronic means of storing and recalling text. The text was thus available for "processing" — revising, merging, moving, etc. Obvious early uses were the production and personalization of form letters.

Text editing was accomplished through coded entries, and was relatively difficult because it was necessary to print out the text each time a change was made to insure that the desired changes had been correctly made. The difficulty was essentially eliminated by the addition of a display screen, a TV-type tube on which all or part of a page was displayed. Using a position indicator, or cursor, it became possible to move around the screen and insert or delete text and immediately view the effect on the whole. It was also possible to scroll back and forth through multipage documents, and in effect perform cut-and-paste editing operations electronically.

Figure 8.1 shows schematically what we will consider the basic word processor. The heart of the device is the computer (central processing unit or CPU) which incorporates the hardware and software (computer programs) that control the operations. Usually, this will also contain the text storage device. Currently the most popular form of storage is the "floppy disc," a plastic disc similar in appearance to a 45 rpm record and capable of storing approximately 100 pages of text. These discs are removable and constitute a library or file of text which can be as large as desired.

The work station in figure 8.1 incorporates the keyboard and a display screen. The keyboard is practically identical with a standard typewriter keyboard, with the addition of special control keys. The control keys are used to perform functions unique to the word processor, such as movement of the cursor, addition or deletion of text and storage, or recall of documents.

The final unit shown in figure 8.1 is a high speed quality printer, i.e., it produces printed output comparable to a fine typewriter. For many word processors, the printer uses a "daisy-wheel" imprinting device. This is a multi-spoke wheel similar in principle to the Selectric typewriter "golf ball," but capable of much faster operation. Daisy wheels are easily changed, and a variety of type styles and sizes are available.

The word processor which has been described is known as a stand-alone unit, i.e., it is complete and incorporates all the necessary functions for text entry, display, editing, printing, storage, and recall. It turns out that in normal operation the printer is not very busy. Text is entered and edited on the screen, and printed copies are produced only at the end for either rough draft or final copy purposes. In addition, when the printer is being used, it is possible to continue to use the work station to prepare other documents at the same time.

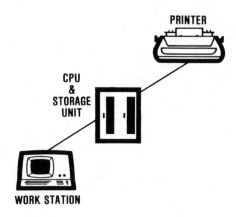

Fig. 8.1. A stand-alone word processor.

The printer is not the only unit being used at less than its capability. This is also true of the CPU. It reacts so quickly to key strokes that most of the time it is in an idle condition. As a result, it is possible to add a second (or more) work station(s) to share the CPU and printer. This is shown schematically in figure 8.2 and is known as a shared logic system. The first and obvious advantage of a shared logic system is economy, the reduced unit costs for each work station because of the sharing of devices. A second and more significant advantage is the ability to share and exchange documents. We will subsequently see how this leads to the integrated network which will constitute the office of the future.

TIP OF THE ICEBERG

We now know enough about word processors to understand how they may be used as the building blocks of the automated office – how they are only the tip of the iceberg, as shown in figure 8.3.

Electronic Files

Up to this point, we have not discussed the reduction or elimination of paperwork as a goal, but it is indeed a valuable end-product to be sought. The importance of using word processors for the preparation of text is that they produce an electronic image of the text which can be displayed and stored. It is this stored electronic image which will become the file copy of the future. We have seen how a shared logic system allows this copy to be shared by multiple work stations. Figure 8.4 shows the addition of a communications link between two shared logic word processors, which in effect extends the capability of file sharing to multiple locations. It thus becomes possible for a single electronic copy to serve as the file copy for all who might have the need to refer to it. A typical study shows that the average business document is distributed to five to six individuals, and that each in turn circulates it to two or three additional persons. Many of these will retain file copies, most of which will never be referred to again. The advantage of replacing these ten to twenty copies with a single copy is obvious from viewpoint of the storage cost alone. This advantage is compounded when we harness the computer power of the system to aid in the retrieval of documents, which is often the most costly aspect of manual files.

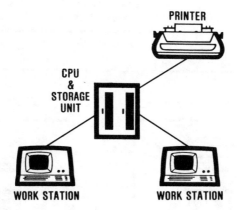

PRINTER

CPU
&
STORAGE
UNIT

WORK STATION   WORK STATION

Fig. 8.2. A shared logic system.

One important consideration in the design of electronic filing systems is security – the files must be reliable, and must be available only to those with the right of access. Another consideration is the need to provide for annotations on documents as they are read by different individuals.

It is likely that a multi-level filing system will simplify some of these considerations. Thus personal files, of interest only to individuals or their immediate associates, would be maintained on the local word processor. A second level of files would contain documents of interest to all at a single location, and would be maintained on a central system at the location. Finally, documents of interest throughout a corporation would be stored at a large computer center accessible to all. This is shown schematically in figure 8.5, which extends the word processor communications link to a larger computer. Retrieval software would be designed to search automatically through the hierarchy of files in a manner transparent to the user.

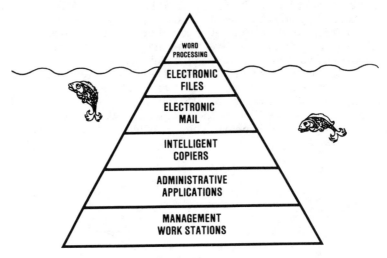

Fig. 8.3. The tip of the iceberg.

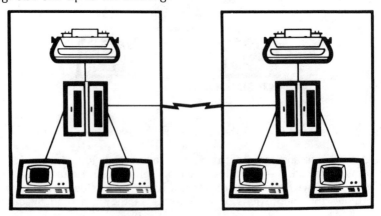

Fig. 8.4. Communicating word processor systems.

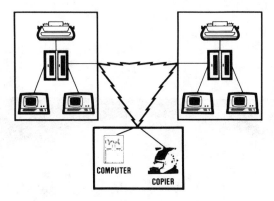

Fig. 8.5. Access to computers and copiers.

Electronic Mail

Early in this paper, productivity gain was cited as the strong motivator for office automation. A key function which will contribute to this is shown on our iceberg in figure 8.3, electronic mail. Electronic mail will promote the rapid and accurate sharing of information among managers – the information which is rapidly becoming the lifeblood of any organization.

Some of the advantages of electronic mail are already widely available in teletype and facsimile systems. These are primarily "once through" systems that result in paper copies at the receiving end. The forwarding of copies requires re-input, and both types of systems suffer from problems of quality and speed. They do offer a great advantage over the regular postal service in much swifter delivery. Also, they are relatively inexpensive.

Linking word processors through telephone lines offers means for accurate and almost instantaneous transmission of documents between any two locations in the world. The development of value-added (retail bandwidths which were bought at wholesale prices) communications networks and satellite communications services will help to promote the cost effectiveness of this activity.

However, electronic mail will not be really effective until everyone is using word processors to produce documents, i.e., it is a critical mass type of activity. In addition, a secondary but significant problem is the need for compatibility between the word processors in the network. Most corporations will solve this problem by limiting their purchase of machines to those of one manufacturer. There is, however, some activity devoted to developing translation devices, and these will be important, especially if electronic mail is to be extended to inter-corporation communications.

Figure 8.6 gives some idea of how an electronic mail/message system will work. It shows the display screen image of an individual's

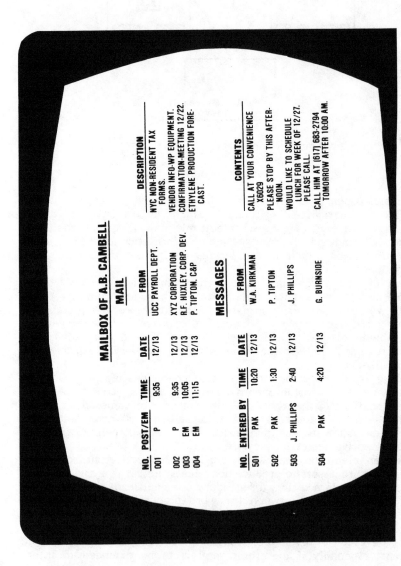

MAILBOX OF A.B. CAMBELL

MAIL

NO.	POST/EM	TIME	DATE	FROM	DESCRIPTION
001	P	9:35	12/13	UCC PAYROLL DEPT.	NYC NON-RESIDENT TAX FORMS.
002	P	9:35	12/13	XYZ CORPORATION	VENDOR INFO-WP EQUIPMENT.
003	EM	10:05	12/13	R.F. HUXLEY. CORP. DEV.	CONFIRMATION-MEETING 12/22.
004	EM	11:15	12/13	P. TIPTON. C&P	ETHYLENE PRODUCTION FORE-CAST.

MESSAGES

NO.	ENTERED BY	TIME	DATE	FROM	CONTENTS
501	PAK	10:20	12/13	W.A. KIRKMAN	CALL AT YOUR CONVENIENCE X6029
502	PAK	1:30	12/13	P. TIPTON	PLEASE STOP BY THIS AFTER-NOON.
503	J. PHILLIPS	2:40	12/13	J. PHILLIPS	WOULD LIKE TO SCHEDULE LUNCH FOR WEEK OF 12/27. PLEASE CALL.
504	PAK	4:20	12/13	G. BURNSIDE	CALL HIM AT (617) 683-2794 TOMORROW AFTER 10:00 AM.

Fig. 8.6. Mailbox display. This illustration gives some idea of how an electronic mail/message system will look. It shows the display screen of an individual's "mailbox". It could be available to the user wherever he/she might be, through a work station connected to the system or through portable work stations at home or on the road.

100

"mail box" which is divided into two categories, mail and messages. The difference between the two is that mail is simply a logging of communications that have been received, whereas the messages are complete in themselves. These latter are the equivalents of the little pink or green slips of papers currently juggled in all the offices of the world. An advantage of the electronic system is that the items will continue to appear until disposed of, and thus can be lost only by intent. It is expected that this type of message system will eliminate many telephone calls currently made.

The mail shown is of two types, electronic mail and postal mail. The logging of electronic mail is accomplished automatically by the system, and the document itself is available at the push of a button. It can be read at the screen and then discarded, forwarded, or filed. The postal mail still represents paper documents which are on the individual's desk, and these represent a real inhibition to an all-electronic system. Text scanners and, ultimately, digital scanners could be used to convert them into electronic form, but eventually the extension of electronic mail to outside mail is the more attractive direction.

An obvious advantage of the electronic mail/message system is that the mailbox will be available to an individual wherever he may be, either through a work station connected to the system or through a portable work station at home or on the road. This is the kind of capability which could significantly affect where and how we do our work.

Many manufacturers are working on the development of electronic mail systems, but these are often limited to stations connected to a single system. The extension to an integrated network of many systems is still to be accomplished.

Intelligent Copier

Next down on the illustrated iceberg is the intelligent copier or image printer. This is, in essence, a high-speed printer rather than a copier, producing paper output directly from the electronic images. Originally developed for use as a computer output device, its value as a word processor output device is equally attractive, allowing the printing of whole pages with variable type styles and sizes intermixed.

Its place in the office of the future is uncertain since it promotes the use of paper copies. However, in the immediate future, while we are still in a transition stage, it will be used. It offers not only the advantages of flexible format but also the value of a remote mail station where multiple copies can be produced from a sending word processor, for distribution at an alternate location.

The first image printers available were very high capacity and very expensive, justifiable by only the largest scale computer operations. Smaller machines more suitable for a typical office environment have begun to appear. These will have an impact in the near future.

Administrative Applications

The next item on our iceberg, labeled administrative applications, refers to the harnessing of the computer power of the word processor itself, or the larger computers it can access, to perform a variety of tasks now done mostly by manual methods.

Many of the current word processors provide software which allows the development of simple computer-type applications such as sorting, mathematics, or decision processing. Recently we have also begun to see the introduction of full-scale computer language compilers. These will allow users to develop their own applications, and will lead the way to a whole host of automated office functions.

Some of these functions will involve merely straightforward translation of current operations, e.g., expense account preparation. The screen will provide a computer-directed form to be "filled" out. The necessary arithmetic will be performed automatically, and the proper accounts will be charged.

Other functions will require interface with existing external computer systems, e.g., rent-a-car services or airlines reservation systems. Instead of calling on the phone, it will be possible to have access to the rent-a-car system directly to reserve a car and receive a confirmation back immediately. Similarly, it will be possible to scan through airline schedules, select desired flights, and purchase and print tickets via the word-processing terminal.

Finally, there will be new kinds of applications which will result in simplified ways of doing things. An example is schedule or calendar maintenance. Figure 8.7 shows the screen image of an individual's calendar for one day. It simply shows the day in half hour segments with appointments noted, as appropriate. The system would maintain data for as far into the future as desired. Ideally, the calendar would be available to all for inspection and scheduling of desired appointments. The greatest advantage will be found when it is necessary to schedule a meeting for a group of individuals. Anyone who has tried to find a mutually acceptable meeting time for five or six people will recognize that it often requires fifteen to twenty phone calls. If their calendars are all maintained on the computer, it will be a relatively simple computer application to scan through the calendars and schedule such a meeting automatically. The system can be as sophisticated as desired. For example, in scheduling such a meeting it can inspect where the individuals are the previous day and not schedule an early meeting if anyone was out of town and would be returning late at night. In the earliest use of such a system, the computer will probably be asked only to propose the scheduled meeting time, and each individual will be contacted to confirm it. People like to maintain close control over something as personal as their own schedules. However, we will eventually see a transition to greater use of automatic scheduling as its value becomes apparent. This is an example of the people-computer interface which will require careful planning to insure acceptance.

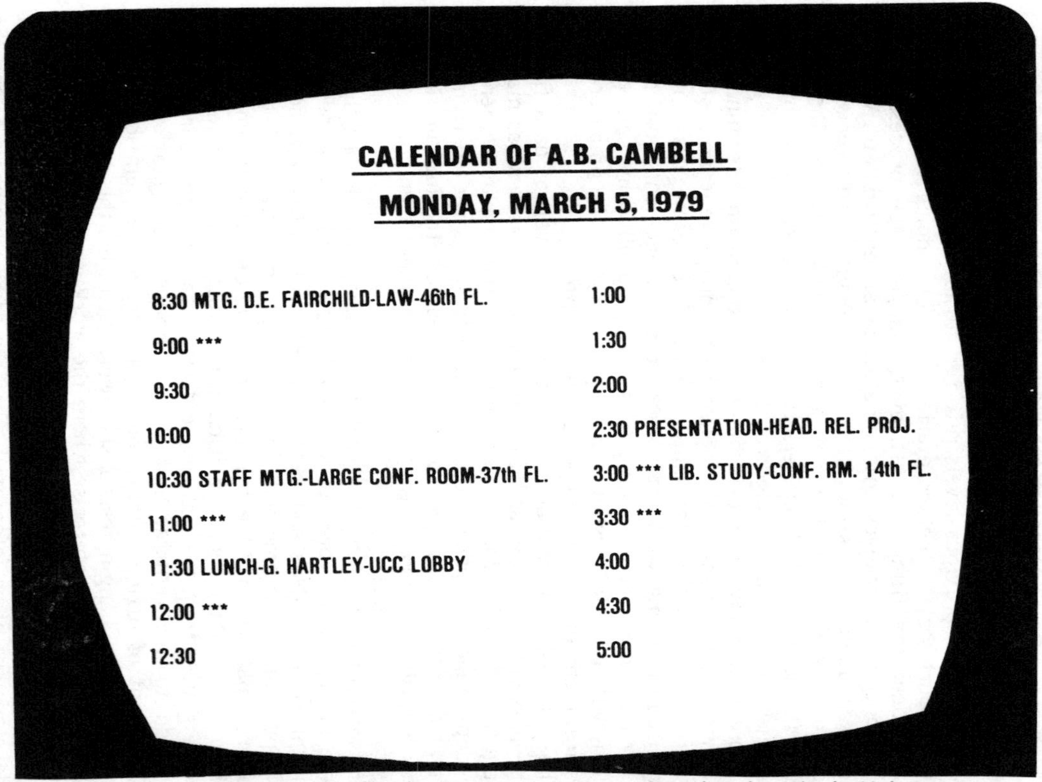

CALENDAR OF A.B. CAMBELL

MONDAY, MARCH 5, 1979

8:30 MTG. D.E. FAIRCHILD-LAW-46th FL.

9:00 ***

9:30

10:00

10:30 STAFF MTG.-LARGE CONF. ROOM-37th FL.

11:00 ***

11:30 LUNCH-G. HARTLEY-UCC LOBBY

12:00 ***

12:30

1:00

1:30

2:00

2:30 PRESENTATION-HEAD. REL. PROJ.

3:00 *** LIB. STUDY-CONF. RM. 14th FL

3:30 ***

4:00

4:30

5:00

Fig. 8.7. Calendar display. It shows an individual's appointments for the day, in half-hour segments. The system would maintain appointments as far into the future as desired, and could schedule meetings for as many people as necessary, meshing their schedules to fit the best available time.

103

The list of possible administrative applications is probably endless. It is certain that as such functions are introduced, the users themselves will find ways to use the available computer power to do things we don't even dream of now.

Management Work Stations

The final level shown on the iceberg is labeled management work stations. All the previous levels referred to activities of the administrative support staff — the secretaries and clerks doing text entry and editing, document filing and retrieval, mail/message processing and distribution, travel arrangements, meeting arrangements, etc. When we introduce management work stations, we place word processor-like stations on the desks of the managers (in the jargon of the trade, principals) and provide them personally with the capability of interacting directly with various electronic systems.

At present, many principals make use of computer terminals, but this is not as significant as the concept of management work stations. They are mainly doing "computer" work — entering data, running programs, interacting with data bases. The management work station will eventually extend this kind of activity to all principals but, in addition, will provide a whole host of new types of computer-based activities, many of them communications-oriented.

The principal will have access to text files as well as data files. It will be possible to access and forward documents as well as mail and messages. Most of these will be viewed on the display screen, with little dependence on paper copies. Data will be extracted from sales results, from forecasts, from production schedules. The information will be incorporated in reports using computer graphic techniques to produce graphs and charts.

The revolutionary aspect of this concept is that the principal will use the management work station in all aspects of his or her work. Communication of ideas and data to others will be fast and accurate. This rapid communication will increase the productivity of the individual principal, which is the true ultimate goal of office automation.

Since many of the most significant advantages of office technology are to be gained from the management work station, some corporations have tried to begin there, that is, to introduce such stations as the starting point of office automation. Apart from the significant problems involved in changing established work patterns, this is likely to be successful only in an enterprise where the work is relatively structured and predictable. In most cases, where the work is less structured and requires creativity, the introduction of work stations will have to await the development of an integrated text-data processing network and the accumulation of files and data bases.

IMPLICATIONS FOR PEOPLE

What are likely to be the effects of the office technologies we have been discussing on people? First of all, since productivity gain is the primary goal, it is expected that fewer people will be required to perform the same amount of work. In the early stages this will first affect the number of support staff, the secretaries and clerks, but will ultimately affect the number of middle-level managers necessary to accomplish the organization's goals.

In a typical large corporation, most managers share secretaries. Depending on the type of work being done, the number sharing a single secretary varies from one or two for managers with many different kinds of typing and administrative needs to as many as ten or twelve for technical groups with minimal support needs. However, in some cases, the actual ratio of managers to secretaries is determined by the status and position of the manager rather than the support needs. The introduction of word processing has provided an opportunity to examine some of these traditional approaches to staffing.

The following simplified analysis will show how word processing has been used to reduce the numbers of support personnel in many organizations. Consider a group of ten managers served by four secretaries, a ratio of 2.5 to 1. Typically each secretary will type 20 to 40 percent of the time. Introducing a single word processing station with its productivity gain would allow all of this typing to be done by one full-time word processing (or correspondence) secretary. Economics would not permit each secretary to have a station which would be used only part-time. In addition, occasional users will not normally acquire skills sufficient to gain the productivity improvement available. Assuming one of the four original secretaries has become the word processing specialist, the three remaining secretaries would divide up the non-typing or administrative tasks, e.g., travel arrangements, meeting scheduling, filing, etc. In most cases, three will be too many for this remaining work and one position can be eliminated. The result is that each of the ten managers is served by two secretaries, the word processing specialist and one of the administrative secretaries. This represents a ratio of 3.33 to 1 or a productivity gain of 33 percent. In terms of dollars, the difference in cost between one secretary and one word processing station will typically result in an annual savings of $10,000 or more. The replication of this example throughout a large organization can thus have a significant financial result.

New Paths for Advancement

There is an alternative scenario, however, which can be even more attractive than reduction in support staff. Instead of eliminating the third administrative secretary, another way of achieving new benefits is by allowing the principals to delegate to the secretaries some of the work they would normally do themselves. It is an unusual manager who doesn't do some work not requiring his or her education and experience which could be delegated to a support worker. This type of delegation has a two-fold benefit – it frees the principal for the more creative aspects of his or her job, and at the same time upgrades the job of the administrative secretary. Ultimately, the potential economic benefit is great, either through reduction in the number of managers required or the increased amount of higher-level work done by them.

The point was made previously that the word processing specialist was spending full-time on the machine. Does this mean that word processing is just the old typing pool but with fancy typewriters? Unfortunately this can be true. Some of the early production-oriented word processing centers have maintained some of the worst aspects of the depersonalized typing pool, with word processing defined as the entry level position to be moved out of as soon as possible. But it does not have to be so. The advanced capabilities of word processing – communications, mathematics, decision processing, programming – all open up the need for the development of a large variety of new skills and the potential for new career paths.

The development of career paths for both administrative and word processing secretaries is an important part of insuring that the office of the future will be a better place to work. Most approaches have considered the multi-level possibilties within both the administrative and word processing tracks, and sought equity of status and compensation so that each track is equally attractive.

One major benefit that can result from this is less dependence of the secretary on the advancement of her boss. With new career paths available, the secretary's advancement can now depend on her own interests and performance. In promoting opportunities for women, most companies have had little trouble in advancing engineers, lawyers, or MBAs, but this has not been the case for the great number of women traditionally relegated to a secretarial "ghetto." Properly applied, office technology will introduce many new career opportunities for them.

These are some of the people-related benefits to be gained in the office of the future. While the reduction in numbers of staff needed is a big attraction to business, it is threatening to those whose jobs will be eliminated. Up to now, most corporations have been able to absorb these reductions through attrition, so that comparatively few people have actually lost jobs as a result of office automation. However, as in manufacturing and agriculture, automation will result in a long-range trend to fewer available jobs. In addition, the jobs available will require higher levels of skill and there will be fewer opportunities for the unskilled. Some new types of jobs, largely service-oriented to help keep the new systems running, will develop, but these too will require relatively high-level skills. The result can be a large number of unemployable people and a profound sociological problem. This paper will not attempt to propose solutions to that problem, but it is important that we begin to recognize the problem before it surfaces, and to seek solutions.

STAGES OF DEVELOPMENT

While it is already possible to acquire suitable equipment to accomplish all of the automated functions discussed, it is not likely that an effort to buy everything at once and install the whole "iceberg" would be successful. Aside from the technical developmental problems in integrating the different functions into a cohesive network, the cultural shock would be overwhelming.

For a typical large corporation with many divisions and locations, a phased approach makes the most sense. This will minimize the shock and provide the opportunity for cost justification at each step. Figure 8.8, Stages of Development, shows a ten-year scenario to illustrate how it might reasonably be accomplished.

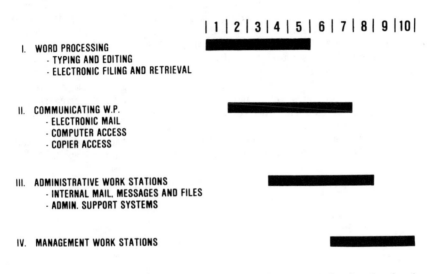

| 1 | 2 | 3 | 4 | 5 | 6 | 7 | 8 | 9 | 10 |

I. WORD PROCESSING
   - TYPING AND EDITING
   - ELECTRONIC FILING AND RETRIEVAL

II. COMMUNICATING W.P.
   - ELECTRONIC MAIL
   - COMPUTER ACCESS
   - COPIER ACCESS

III. ADMINISTRATIVE WORK STATIONS
   - INTERNAL MAIL, MESSAGES AND FILES
   - ADMIN. SUPPORT SYSTEMS

IV. MANAGEMENT WORK STATIONS

| 1 | 2 | 3 | 4 | 5 | 6 | 7 | 8 | 9 | 10 |
YEAR

Fig. 8.8. Stages of development.

Stage I, the word processing stage, extends for five years and represents the acquisition of word processors essentially for the basic functions of typing and editing. During these eary days it is possible to begin some initial efforts at electronic filing and retrieval, primarily for local files.

As soon as a number of word processors are installed, it makes sense to begin to tie them together through communications for document exchange. This is Stage II and lags shortly behind Stage I. During this period, the rudiments of electronic mail will be developed. In addition there will be access to computers to extract data to be incorporated in reports. During this stage there will continue to be dependence on paper copies so that access to intelligent copiers also will be attractive.

After three years or so, there will begin to be an accumulation of electronically-filed material, and it will be appropriate to begin to acquire administrative work stations for non-word processing applications. It is during this Stage III that electronic mail message systems will begin to have a serious impact. It will also be possible to extend the files beyond the local level. Finally the administrative support systems such as scheduling, travel arrangements, etc. will be developed and implemented. It is during this Stage III that the ambiance of the office of the future will really begin to be felt.

The final Stage IV corresponds to the introduction of management work stations which extend access to all the systems directly to the manager at his or her own desk. This will become the principal's prime communication link and source of information. Sophisticated computer and graphics capability will also be available for use with the text and data files which constitute the information library. It is at this stage that the major benefits will accrue.

Although this development scenario was designed for relatively large organizations, its principles will apply to groups of any size. It will always be appropriate to follow some type of phased approach to minimize cost and cultural problems. The office of the future offers many wonders and benefits. The careful planning required to insure that these benefits are actually achieved is a worthwhile investment.

9 Some Questions about the New Office Technology

James M. West

Before we become too enamored of "the office of the future," which has been receiving a lot of enthusiastic publicity lately, I'd like to list a few caveats. I want to consider the "people impact" of the new technology, and whether the new devices are as important as they are made to appear.

When we talk about efforts to bring greater productivity in the office, we're really talking about two things. There's an initial step that every user goes through in "upgrading" the everyday office environment. That step is mechanization. You find you are unable to do very much about the frustrating volume of paperwork. You feel that if you mechanize, you'll be able to capture and confine that paperwork ogre, and at the same time make the new machines perform a number of utility chores for you, such as paper communication, visual on a terminal, while you perhaps do the editing or revising, with some kind of printing device to do the typing. Now you have merely mechanized what was formerly done manually.

The office of the future is a level beyond that — it is automated. That is the second step. The distinction between mechanizing and automating lies in the measure of control that moves from the person to the machine. This might be exemplified by the way an executive's calendar is kept. The secretary, who is charged with maintaining the schedule, performs all of the notations manually. You can mechanize that. You can put the schedule on a device of some sort. But unless that device automatically does more for you than merely keeping the schedule — like providing the itinerary for travel, maybe making your reservations and even printing your tickets — unless the machine does these things, you really haven't automated. You haven't gained very much.

THE BENEFITS AREN'T THERE

We are anticipating a lot of benefits in the office of the future, and attempting to get them from mechanizing processes. We are not reaping many of the expected benefits. Instead, we find that we are upsetting the order of the way things get done in the office. Any number of organizations can recite any number of sad experiences, beginning with word processing. What has happened is that we have mistakenly sold an automation label, while we have simply mechanized.

What we're attempting to do in the context of office systems is to determine ways to link up the various items of hardware. When we talk about a non-display typewriter, I can start most easily by saying it's a non-something, it's a non-display, it's hard copy. The difficulty there is the number of repetitions we have to go through before finally producing a usable piece of communication. The biggest problem we see is in materials called, in our operation, code prints. They contain both the machine instructions and the ultimate communication. You cannot look into the text at one particular point. To locate something within twenty pages, you must play all the twenty pages to find the paragraph you are seeking. That takes us to the necessity of finding how to reach data more quickly, hone in on the precise segment of information we want.

The Terminal

The other benefit – we are seeking this on most of the terminal devices associated with office processing – is that on one display screen we are seeing a partitioned window which gives us both the code instructions telling us where we are, what file we're in, and a "menu" to determine what we want to do with this material. Then on the bottom half of the screen, perhaps, we see the rest of the material.

Eyesight, Office "Landscaping"

There is a degree of employee concern over eye fatigue when using a terminal all day. (When you get technically into the terminals, there is an entirely different field of human factors engineering. Being debated as of 1979 and 1980, when the Fairfield University seminars on communication were taking place, were such matters as whether the dark character is better against the white background or a white character against a dark background.) Many display systems are sold with the idea that the employee will be physically looking at the display device all day. That normally does not happen and should not happen, any more than a preparer of documents looks at a typewriter carriage all the time. When you do it every day you don't look at any particular fixed point.

There is considerable debate concerning what these questions mean to the technical plans for the office, and they link closely with office landscaping, and with the layout of the modern office. We talk about lighting, task lighting and ambient lighting, ambient referring to the ceiling lights or the general lights available in a room. We have directed our designers to place display devices at various distances from employees who are going to use them, and then we wonder why these employees either can't see what's on the screen or why the lights appear to be wrong. That's a particular problem we must examine in terms of the spacing of desks, the way items are laid out, and the kind of lighting that is best for the purpose.

We expect to see a continuing trend in open-space office land-scaping. This usually means partitions five or six feet high, not completely to the ceiling, and built-in furniture nestled around those partitions. There's a cost that goes with it, but there is also a use argument that says if the office landscaping is designed correctly, it can be a powerful offset to costs in the cost-benefit ratio.

FEAR OF CHANGE

One of the things you hear a great deal about in any proposed arrangement is the resistance to change. People now coming through colleges and universities are fairly familiar with an office keyboard, computer keyboard, or terminal keyboard and data on visual display. But most people in offices did not have that advantage in the years when it was first possible to experiment with these new devices. We find that along with the typical job pressures, we seem to be picking up a fear of the changing office environment. Much has been written about this, but very little that tells us how to cope with the problem.

I'll give you a thesis I'm trying to develop: I believe the biggest issue in the resistance to change is the fear of losing control. I use the word "control" in the broadest sense. At the high managerial levels, it means loss of financial control, that is, the business is going to get away from us, and before we know it we'll have big problems. That's certainly one aspect of control. A small analogy of control is this: you have an alarm clock that wakes you up every morning. If someone were coming to your bedside every thirty days or every three months suggesting you try this new bigger and better alarm clock, I think you'd have a problem with that, too. Particularly if it didn't work one morning and didn't wake you up.

How do you maintain control over the activities of your particular operation? How do you manage your people? During staff meetings? If so, maybe electronic mail and fewer staff meetings is not that exciting to you. Maybe, if you send an electronic message to someone and you don't get a response, nothing happens. Maybe the message wasn't even received. You'd feel you're losing control and I don't think you'd be a very enthusiastic proponent of electronic mail. Perhaps you have other control measures and you've learned to make them work. They may not be perfect, but they get the job done. Here come the engineers, or the technical community, or the systems community (as some of them like to be called), asking you to try this new solution. If they have not duplicated your controls, or at least installed equivalent controls in the new system, I think it's going to be a problem for you. I read over and over that we're afraid of change, yet the rate of entry products into the office, as well as the entire computer environment, suggests that we have handled changes much better than contemporary writers on the office of the future would have you believe.

OPENER TO THE FUTURE OFFICE

One of the topics I want to deal with is the terminology that's developing about "the office of the future." Just what does that phrase mean? It's not very descriptive. It probably conceals more than it reveals. There is not a specific point in time when the augmentation of communication devices places you in the office of the future. You don't come from the office of the past to the office of the present to the office of the future with that most recent electronic device you have purchased.

I think we are beginning to approach that point with something called, generically, a multifunction work station. That work station is able to function in a free-standing mode. It's driven usually by a minicomputer or a microcomputer, depending upon whose technology it has and how recent it is. Typically, it has gateways to various communication networks. It is characterized by a document-creation device to capture key strokes and to capture graphics. More important, it is able to produce a variety of printing outputs. Using terminal devices and the basic display devices, it may be given a command to print or to create hard copy or to send a message. I think that is going to be the beginning of the multifunction work station — that's an opener to the office of the future.

Some of the ways these devices are used apply to a method of sending messages which presumably is more satisfactory than traveling to meetings, or teleconferencing, or other situations, because those methodologies require that two or more people interrupt whatever else they are doing, and actually get together. With message-switching devices, you can file your message today through terminal displays and if the reader comes in on the receiving end, you will have your response by tomorrow.

There is a question as to how instantaneous this will ever become, because of a human pattern — taking a little time before making a decision. If you want a yes-no answer on an issue of fact, maybe you can get that through network switching, literally in an instant. If, however, it is something that requires normal contemplation of, say, a business proposal, the most sophisticated electronics will not make that answer come through more rapidly — you might have to sleep on it. In any event, the technology is there when that answer is available.

Electronic mail will come into this kind of a work station. Virtually everything is inspected on the display device.

One of the questions that has arisen is the degree to which an executive (I class that word rather loosely to mean anyone from unit manager to the chairman of the board) will want to be involved in an advanced system. One of the alternatives – and I think we'll probably try to go this way, at least initially – is to familiarize the secretarial support staff totally with a full-function station that types, makes copies, and edits typewritten copy. I believe we will put a kind of auxiliary terminal, a display device, in the executive's office. Probably nothing more, not a keyboard, not a controlling mechanism, just the visual display device. The executive will work through the secretary as usual. But instead of saying "Get me a piece of paper out of the file" or "Go down to the library," he will ask the secretary to bring the thing up on the screen so he can take a look at it. Then, if editing changes or revisions are required, there would be discussions between the secretary and the executive. But the secretary retains control of the keyboard and actually puts the documents in. I believe that's the way it will begin.

We obviously have options to go beyond that. For example, we would allow a "read only upon command" button, controlled by the executive, but it makes the secretaries pretty nervous when we talk about letting the boss into the live files. This is one of the issues that gets in the way of the utility and cost-effectiveness of such equipment.

I find that when I talk to people in the office, I have to begin with the word processing kind of environment. I find executives not unwilling to invest some money on experimenting with different kinds of hardware. That's not to say that any manufacturer has an easy game as far as the cost of a particular product is concerned. But when we're talking about the difference between hiring another secretary versus making a commitment to hardware, it appears that managers can almost work with the amount they would have to depreciate each year. Whether to buy hardware or add a full-time employee year round becomes a serious matter for decision. One of the issues, though, is this: if the new gadget doesn't do enough, if it can be useful only two or three hours a day, there's little hope for its remaining in place. Which takes me to this business of the advanced multifunction.

MULTIFUNCTION

An acquaintance of mine recently drew a comparison between the "idiot lights" on one of these so-called advanced design automobiles and the computer. You know those idiot lights, of course: the parking lights on, you're informed by a light on the dashboard; the oil pressure is wrong, you get it by a light; the brake is not fully released, you get a light; the high beams are on, you get a whole readout right across a small, perhaps six-inch long, strip of indicator lights. That analogy can be taken into the computer environment and certainly into the office of the future by an approach which says: We set a plan, we set a target. Perhaps we depend literally on colored lights, if we are able to have the color technology; or we depend on symbols.

Let's say twenty different business organizations are in a gigantic corporation, and let's assume nineteen of them are "on plan." Only number 20 requires our attention. We get a warning signal. To continue this example: All the parts of the big corporation are "on plan" – that's a green light. Or a symbol meaning "I'm OK, you don't have to look at me." Perhaps yellow light or some equivalent symbol would mean, "We're within a few points of making plans, maybe 4 percent below." A red light symbol would mean "We are off the plan and here's what we have to look for."

That's a simple example. Some companies have already gone a distance toward setting up some such information technology. My point is simply that this is the kind of information of which the executive is woefully short. The executive has, in volume, all the information, in fact, more than he can use. He can request any kind of information he wants. It is the knowledge arising from that information that we are slow to be able to handle. Many organizations fight the problem of workload by saying, "Well, the only way I'm going to answer this problem is to allocate ten more accountants," or whatever. This is where the idea of the office of the future has a role to play. It is by highlighting information, either process-oriented or communications-oriented. The executive reasons: "I've got a problem in this area, I've got to look much deeper here, but I do not have a problem in three other areas, so I don't need to spend three nights this week just determining that I'm on target." What this requires is the ability to link the technology of the communication system and the science of systems management and, when necessary, the behavioral sciences.

Once it all gets there, will it be used? And will it be used for the purpose intended, or does it force people to operate in entirely different ways? If it does, we will find that either managers or secretaries will use some portion of the benefits but they will never use it all.

The Electronic Telephone

One area that is proving interesting – and it relates to the office of the future in an indirect way – is the electronic telephone system, eliciting a behavioral reaction that ranges from one extreme to the other. One is a feeling of insult that you would even suggest taking people to school to use a telephone, because they've only been using it all their lives; the other is an attitude of sheer panic when people in a pressure situation cannot actuate the signal devices that are different from those of the standard electromechanical telephone. If you're powerful enough in the organization you tell the engineers to get the damn gadgets out of here, and you go look for another kind of electronic telephone system.

Whatever the system, it can be linked with many of the display devices that are just on the horizon and in the hardware stage. For example, a company might have a manual directory of names and addresses used by some of its top people. It includes the names of contacts made at trade shows, people inside the company, the tailor down the street, the dry cleaner, the barber, and everything else –

4,000 names. One of the first link-ups will be to mount this where it can be seen on a display device, where a precise name can be picked out. Another item some scientific people are trying to make is a gadget which will dial a telephone when a finger is pointed at it. That's an example of multifunction.

NO BONANZAS

One of my views is this: any of these devices, if it performs only one or two chores, such as printing a piece of paper or introducing a certain number of keystrokes into a disk and does only that, will probably not be of much use in an office of the future. It will not result in helping reduce costs by reducing workforce. Most companies, frankly, are too smart to make such reductions anyway. They have been careful to watch the growth of secretarial and support staffs. So, the new communication devices are unlikely to produce the kind of bonanzas that were once touted when the computer made its entrance into areas where there were literally thousands of clerks doing very structured and easily mechanized work.

There are more clerical workers today than ever before. So if we're not going to pick up a lot of savings in reduction of personnel, what we're really talking about is increasing the speed, the turn-around, the accuracy, and the general utility of the work we're attempting to do. The new systems are going to prove valuable to you if you can draft a letter, turn around five minutes later to inquire into the status of your order file, reaching into the depths of another system that runs perhaps on different equipment, talk to that order file, next perhaps generate the data for a memo you're going to write. Then you are actually accessing part of the data processing environment.

10 Applying New Communication Technologies in Canada: A Case Study

J. Raymond Marchand

It is one thing to develop a concept, translate it into a model and into a prototype, and make one-of-a-kind units. It is quite another, and crucially important, to build on the concept and develop the second step. This involves (a) demonstrating technical feasibility, that is, the ability of the gadget to tolerate the real world, and (b) teaching people how to use it for their benefit.

I propose to describe two demonstration projects illustrating the application of the new communication techology.

DEMONSTRATION PROJECTS

The first of these projects is a fiber optics field trial. The scientific and popular press has in recent years provided much information about fiber optics field trials. Most fiber optics installations today are for trunking purposes, that is, for carrying bundles of information between two points, as for example between two telephone exchanges. These are important applications, but there is another use of fiber technology. That is in the network where you are interfacing between the exchange and the subscriber, in what we call the local loop. That is technologically a little more stringent. When you are connecting two exchanges, you are working in a somewhat protected environment, but when you're out there in the field, you are exposing the technology to the vagaries of climate, among other things, and of people too, for that matter.

There are "in the works" a number of fiber optics field trials of the kind I'm describing. One, in Japan, is well along toward completion. Three others happen to be in Canada, two in urban settings, one rural. Why would anybody in his right mind want to try this in a rural setting? To answer that question I must briefly describe an operation in Canada called the Rural Communication Program. Forty kilometers west of

Winnipeg, in central Canada, is a small town called Elie, Manitoba. It contains about 300 people. In that town and in the surrounding farming district, we intend to conduct our field trial.

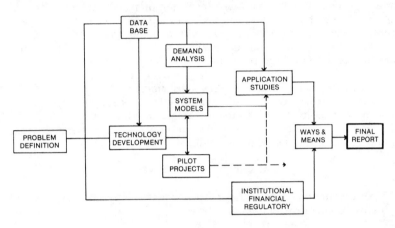

Fig. 10.1. Technological studies and developments involved in creating a communication system for rural Canada, from problem definition to final report.

What are our motivations? Some 27% of the Canadian population consists of rural residents, yet there is a tremendous urban-rural gap in communication. By rural we mean towns whose population is 2,500 or less, or small settlements, or even no town at all. In these areas there are still many households which are enjoying, if I may use the word loosely, four-party phone service. In some parts of the country, there are as many as nine parties to a line. One might reasonably ask, "Why are rural communications so bad?" It's because in rural areas the cost of distribution goes up dramatically. The Canadian Rural Communications Program is seeking to overcome these economic obstacles, and to see whether, through new technology or through more ingenious use of existing technologies, we might be able to break the cost barrier. We are undertaking a variety of experiments, among them being the application of fiber optics. When will we make our breakthrough? Perhaps in '83, perhaps '84 or '86 or '87, some day in the not-too-distant future.

To install a fiber will not cost any more than installing a copper wire. The difference is this: with the fiber you can probably triple the revenue base. That is what we are counting on to provide rural communication of a better quality.

One of our objectives in the field trial is the need to accelerate usage in order to bring forward the date at which high-level utilization and production will lead to lower prices. This is understandable if you try to see how common carriers operate. Common carriers are under pressure, political and other, to improve service. They can't just wait until fiber optics technology is ready. Every day they have to spend more money to provide better service, or simply to keep up with the demand. And of course, they are investing money in current technology which will later have to be replaced. So the sooner we can come up with something better, the sooner we will be able to effect some of the necessary savings. The basic services we have to provide over this system in order to bridge the urban-rural gap are these:

- single-party telephone for every subscriber;
- eight or nine video channels, available from nearby Winnipeg;
- seven FM radio channels, also available in Winnipeg;
- a basic data capability which will allow us in a second stage to undertake a number of new service experiments.

Table 10.1. Objectives.

1. Test the application of fiber optics technology under real environmental and operational conditions;

2. Assess the technical and economic feasibility of utilizing fiber optics technology for improving communications services in rural areas;

3. Provide Canadian industry with an incentive to develop a domestic systems capability in fiber optics technology;

4. Provide both government and the industry with technical, economic, and marketing data required for possible decisions in respect to policies, regulatory requirements, and future systems choices.

One of the interesting developments is our use of a single fiber from a distribution center to the home. On that fiber the householder will have his individual telephone line, his single TV channel, his seven FM radio channels, and a sophisticated information capability.

The way you select your TV channel is by remote control. In other words, there's a basic divergence here from cable TV as we have it today, where all the channels arrive at your home and you switch on the channel you want. Ours is a remote switching situation which, in the context of the level of fiber development in the early 80s, is more economical. Maybe later, when multiplexing techniques or wavelength multiplexing becomes feasible, it will be possible to do the same thing as you do on Coax, but that is not a limitation. (Multiplexing is a technique permitting the simultaneous transmission of several channels of communications – telephone circuit, TV channels, etc. – over the same medium.) The important thing is to be able to do your own thing and get the program you want.

Just to be sure, a second spare fiber will be installed, because, after all, this is a field trial. If we knew that everything would be all right, we wouldn't need a field trial. That second fiber can be used to bring a second TV channel into the home or to indulge in some video-interactive communications.   Alternatively, the second TV channel could be put on the first fiber. These are some examples of the kind of services we would like to play around with in this system. We are limited only by our imagination.

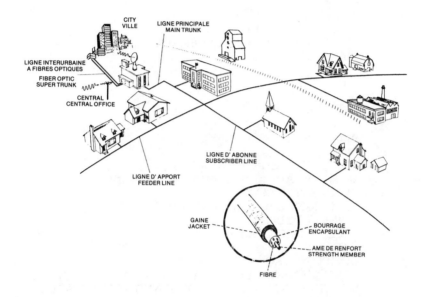

Fig. 10.2. Field trial – information lines extending urban to rural.

The Transmission Problem

One of my pet viewpoints about communication of the future is that we should try as engineers to solve the transmission problem once and for all. Today we build a house and we install what is, for all practical purposes, unlimited sewage disposal, unlimited water supply, unlimited electricity – all the householder might ever need. I think that someday we should also have, probably by way of fiber optics, unlimited communication. Transmission would no longer be an impediment. You would be limited only by your imagination and by the ability to pay for the products of that imagination.

The field trial is going to cost about $5 million in its initial stage. That's a lot of money for 150 subscribers, but this is not a commercial proposition. It's one of those cost-insensitive demonstrations whose purpose is to get across an idea and a service. The $5 million required is being provided on a 50-50 basis by the government and the Canadian Telecommunications Carriers Association. We believe that this participation by the industry is very important and indicative of their eventual willingness to utilize the benefits of the new technology.

Table 10.2. New Home and Business Services

VIDEO: CATV*
          PAY-TV
          EDUCATIONAL TV
          TV ON DEMAND (VIDEO LIBRARY)
          VIDEO CONFERENCING
          TELE-MEDICINE
          VIDEOPHONE

AUDIO: TELEPHONE*
          FM RADIO*
          AM RADIO*

DATA: FIRE AND SECURITY ALARMS
          METER READING AND POWER SHEDDING
          ELECTRONIC MAIL
          ELECTRONIC BANKING AND SHOPPING
          OPINION POLLING
          ELECTRONIC GAMES
          FACSIMILE
          COMPUTER ACCESS
          FARM MANAGEMENT SERVICES
          WEATHER, NEWS, COMMODITY AND STOCK MARKET
          CLASSIFIED ADS, DINING AND ENTERTAINMENT
          TIMETABLES, ETC.
          REFERENCE AND LIBRARY INFORMATION

*These currently available services are included for completeness

The 'Anik' Brothers

Now, to another program, which we call the Anik B Program. Canada has a satellite system called Anik. Anik means "brother" in Eskimo. There are two "brothers," Anik A, the older one, and now Anik B. The present generation of satellites uses the four and the six Gigahertz band (4/6 GHz) as U.S. satellites and INTELSAT do. Anik B, successor and supplementor of Anik A, is more sophisticated, having four transponders in the twelve and fourteen Gigahertz bands, so as to take advantage of more recent technology. Involved in our work are both socially-oriented projects and technical ones. We hope that these will translate into everyday services.

This whole concept of pilot projects originated with what at one time was called the CTS satellite, more recently renamed Hermes. This is a high-powered communications satellite suitable for direct-to-home broadcasting which was developed jointly by NASA and the Canadian Department of Communications on a 50-50 basis and launched by NASA. This satellite was the harbinger of many new experiments in Canada and in the United States. Anik B will utilize the same bands in the upper part of the spectrum in order to go one step further in providing the same kind of new services, maybe under different conditions using a lower power.

These are some of the milestones relating to the Anik B program. It started in 1972 when a Memorandum of Understanding between NASA and Canada was signed dealing with the Hermes satellite, the high-powered one. Later it led to another step towards programming the useful life of Anik B, which was launched on December 7, 1978. Leasing the four transponders cost Canadians $34 million over two years. In addition, approximately $4 million was budgeted to help various organizations undertake experiments of their choice.

In the twelve and fourteen Gigahertz bands, the satellite covers Canada through four spot beams. There are two reasons for that. First, we economize on power when we use a narrower beam; secondly, it affords an opportunity for regional differentiation in programming material and permits taking into account different time zones. (This satellite would cover most of Canada through these four spot beams at twelve and fourteen Gigahertz.) The lower frequency beam continues to cover all of Canada, particularly the north, in order to supplement the service presented provided by Anik A.

Tele-Medicine, Tele-Education

We divided the program into a number of specific geographical areas. There is an emphasis on tele-medicine and tele-education. In addition, the system carries communications originated by and produced by native peoples, American Indian and Eskimo. In Ontario, a number of tele-education experiments are being undertaken. The Ontario Educational Communications Authority is interested in using the satellite to bring to the northland the education facilities available in the south. Moreover, the Ontario provincial government is interested in using the satellite to see how effective it might be for provincial government communications. Some communications projects have been initiated by the Eskimos living in northern Quebec. In the Atlantic region and in the maritime provinces, a number of experiments involving universities are under way. And in Arctic Canada we are developing social experiments with the help of the Eskimo people. There is keen interest among the members of this group of Eskimos who want to communicate with other Eskimos in northern Quebec. As you can see, the common carriers are heavily involved, as well as Telesat Canada, the organization providing domestic satellite service, and Teleglobe, our overseas communications organization, which utilizes both satellites and transcontinental cables.

The overall expectations of all these experiments is that at some point somebody will be convinced that they are feasible, that they are economically viable; and that somebody will then take the initiative to start providing the resulting services on an everyday basis. Then we will see the concepts becoming a part of the real world.

An interesting scenario, I think, is the marriage of these two technologies for rural and remote Canada. It's easy to conceive that the satellite could be used, for example, to provide a basic program package of, say, twelve channels to all of Canada. By doing that, the individual usage costs become extremely low. The basic package would become available everywhere, in cities, small towns, villages, hamlets, possibly even a big ranch. A distribution center could receive this basic package, add to it whatever programming or other news services they could conjure up, and then redistribute the whole package via fiber optics to individual homes and businesses.

11 Smart Machines Learn to See, Talk, Listen, Even "Think" For Us

Richard M. Restak

According to a joke making the rounds among computer specialists, a computer programmed for evaluating interplanetary space travel was once asked to assess the chances for success of a proposed manned-space vehicle completing a round-trip voyage between Earth and Venus. The interrogation, which required several hours to program into the computer, took place, so the story goes, deep within the bowels of the Pentagon and was carried out in the presence of some of the nation's top military advisers.

At the completion of the arduous programming procedure the programmer, along with the visiting VIPs, sat back and waited expectantly for the computer's decision. Within seconds the computer responded, "Yes." The programmer, unsatisfied with such a response to a series of complex and multilayered questions, impatiently retorted, "Yes, what?" to which the computer meekly replied, "Yes, sir!"

The prospects of a computer sophisticated enough to incorporate concepts of military protocol along with specialized knowledge about space flight isn't nearly as ludicrous as this apocryphal tale suggests. Computers are already capable of playing championship chess, helping to avert airline disasters, or prospect for oil; they even conduct some psychotherapy sessions. Each of these is an example of "artificial intelligence" (AI), defined by M.I.T.'s Marvin Minsky as "the science of making machines do things that would require intelligence if they were done by men."

And as with any new field, artificial intelligence and computer science research are raising perplexing and troubling questions. Can machines be developed that are smarter than their human creators? Will artificial intelligence make the human brain obsolete?

In rapid and accurate arithmetic calculations, for instance, a $20 hand-held calculator can already outperform the human brain, and there is little likelihood that the brain will ever narrow this gap. So the questions have already been answered in the affirmative, at least in regard to rapid calculation.

But arithmetic is obviously only a tiny part of the human brain's capabilities. Even something as seemingly simple as recognizing a friend's face involves the convergence of thousands of parallel circuits interconnecting in ways that are, so far, impossible in the linear "on-off" system of a computer.

Some recent efforts have attempted to combine the computer's rapid processing time with the brain's superior talent for pattern recognition. One area in which this hybrid approach is proving successful is speech recognition. Experts have long recognized the advantages of a machine that could communicate by voice rather than by the present system which uses a typewriter-like keyboard. Such a system would be more appealing because most people communicate verbally, and it would probably be more efficient.

At IBM's Thomas J. Watson Research Center in Yorktown Heights, New York, I observed a demonstration of automatic speech recognition which could be common in the office of the future. Dr. N. Rex Dixon, one of the principal researchers in IBM's speech-recognition work, started off by speaking the letters of the alphabet and the digits zero through nine into a microphone connected to a computer terminal. At this point the speech-recognition device was ready to go. A moment later, after Dixon spoke my name into the microphone, "Richard M. Restak," correctly spelled, appeared on the viewing screen.

Although continuous speech-recognition systems have a long way to go before shorthand and typewriters disappear from offices, scientists at IBM predict that in the not-too-distant future inexpensive speech-recognition machines may be available to take dictation of a letter and produce a draft within a few seconds.

Just as each person possesses a distinct fingerprint, so, too, individual speech can be analyzed into unique components. This may allow a person to carry out banking transactions someday simply by making a telephone call and talking to the bank's voice verifier, which will have a record of the individual's voice pattern. Some experts are even speculating that if automatic voice verifiers become popular enough, our present reliance on handwritten signatures could give way to a system where we "signed" important documents over the phone.

While some computers are listening to us, others are learning to talk. Computer-driven voice synthesizers are finding dramatic application among the blind and visually handicapped. Kurzweil Computer Products of Cambridge, Massachusetts, has developed a computer capable of reading books aloud. The device is already in use at the Library of Congress. When a book is opened and placed face down on top of a scanner, letters on the page are converted to digital signals that are analyzed by a small computer and transformed into speech by an electronic voice synthesizer. Unlike the monotonous voice of earlier speech synthesizers, the Kurzweil Reading Machine (KRM) can vary the emphasis on particular sounds in a manner similar to natural spoken English. Programmed with 2,500 pronunciation "rules," the KRM is capable of emphasizing some words more than others, and pausing at various times to avoid "machinelike" speech. The KRM controls the synthesizer's sound-producing circuits in much the same way the human brain controls the jaw, tongue, and throat muscles in order to shape the vocal tract for the production of human speech.

But using speech obviously depends on more than just acoustical processing. There are rules of grammar and syntax that all of us learn and that presumably could be learned by an intelligent machine. If a five-year-old can carry out a reasonably comprehensible conversation with his mother, why can't a multimillion-dollar computer do as well? An intelligent machine, if it is to understand ordinary language, must be capable of drawing inferences: "I had a headache this morning; before I got relief I had to go to three drugstores." Implicit in this sentence is the speaker's failure to find a headache-relieving medicine in the first two drugstores. How can a machine draw such a conclusion since it is unable to have a headache and has never had the experience of visiting a drugstore?

Scientists at Yale University's Artificial Intelligence Laboratory are developing ways to supply computers with the background they need to draw inferences. According to the laboratory director, Dr. Roger L. Schank, much of human behavior is dependent on people learning large numbers of "scripts," shorthand versions of common everyday activities. By supplying computers with a variety of basic scripts, researchers have already produced intelligent machines with information systems which, although limited to specialized areas, can draw inferences and reach conclusions as intelligently as humans.

A dramatic example is SUMEX, a biomedical resource computer funded by the National Institutes of Health and based at the Stanford Medical School in Stanford, California. Among some 20 AI projects in medicine now linked to SUMEX are the following:

- SECS, an AI project at the University of California, Santa Cruz, is now helping chemists design the syntheses of complex, biologically important substances. A spinoff of this program predicts possible cancer-causing effects from the metabolism of compounds foreign to the human body, such as pesticides or food dyes and preservatives.
- MYCIN, a computer program at the Stanford Medical School, is able to review with a physician the patients' symptoms and then provide suggestions for further testing, diagnosis, and treatment. MYCIN can answer questions and, upon request, it can explain its reasoning pattern in order to acquaint the doctor with the basis for coming up with its own suggestions.
- INTERNIST, a medical computer project at the University of Pittsburgh, aids internists in the solution of complex diagnostic problems. At present, the program deals with nearly 500 diseases and more than 3,000 individual manifestations of disease. While designed for use by physicians, it is also expected to provide help to physicians' assistants in remote rural health clinics, to corpsmen in submarines, and maybe even to astronauts on future space missions.

Artificial intelligence processes are also being applied to the study of games such as chess, backgammon, and checkers, and, in at least one instance, results have been impressive. A computer program, the brainchild of Dr. Hans Berliner of Carnegie-Mellon University in Pittsburgh, defeated the 1979-80 World Backgammon Champion, Paul Magriel, 7-to-1, in a seven-point challenge match. Ironically, the unseated champion was one of the consultants contributing to the development of the victorious program.

The outlook for a counterpart becoming champion in the ethereal realm of international chess is at the moment more controversial. When chess-playing computer programs were developed in the mid-1950s, enthusiasts confidently predicted that within a decade a computer program would become the world champion. It has yet to appear on the scene despite continually updated predictions of its imminent arrival. This may be due, in part, to the different ways computers and highly skilled human players go about playing the game.

At any given point in a chess game, the number of possible responses carried out three moves ahead for each side is, for all practical purposes, infinite. With high-speed microelectronic circuits, a chess computer like the one at Bell Labs in Murray Hill, New Jersey, can evaluate some 5,000 positions per second. But for the fastest of modern computers to calculate even ten moves ahead for each side, considering all possibilities, it would take tens of thousands of years.

Skilled human players are highly discriminating in the types of moves they consider. Instead of mentally "trying out" large numbers of potential moves, the superior player concentrates on evaluating a small number of promising ones. The very top players seem to employ highly original, intuitive, and idiosyncratic methods of playing which, in many cases, they do not even understand themselves.

Lubomir Kavalek, who is the current reigning American chess champion, guesses that a chess computer costing less than $200 soon will be able to defeat all but the best chess players in the world. "But these people," he says, "I don't think will ever be beaten by a computer."

Although so far checkmated at world championship chess, the accomplishments of AI and computer science in many other fields are already well beyond the most ambitious speculations of a decade ago.

Natural and man-made disasters are now being successfully simulated by computer. During the crisis at Three Mile Island, computers were able within days to estimate the extent of damage to the fuel elements inside the nuclear reactor core, providing urgently needed information. In another recent application, a computer in Boulder, Colorado, aided a 75-member team of specialists in their attempt to predict and control the patterns of oil spillage on the Texas coast from a runaway offshore Mexican oil well.

It takes a computer to catch a crook

In New York City a special police unit, CATCH (Computer-Assisted Terminal Criminal Hunt), is in operation to aid in the rapid identification of criminal suspects. The unit can selectively scan photographs and information on some 250,000 suspects arrested within the past three years. Initially, detectives question a crime victim about 45 descriptive features of the criminal. Answers are then fed into the system which correlates the identified characteristics. Finally, the computer prints out the photographs of the most likely suspects for the purpose of identification.

Airline pilots are now able to simulate take-off and landing experiences, using computer models. While sitting at a set of mock controls, the pilots start with the simulation of everyday flight experiences and then quickly graduate to challenges they rarely encounter in day-to-day routines. A commercial pilot can interact with computer simulations of the behavior of powerful airplanes that travel at supersonic speeds. Or, simulations can be devised of airline catastrophes for the purposes of determining alternative, possibly more successful performances. (Computer simulation of the May 25, 1979, Chicago air disaster in which 273 persons died, for instance, revealed that even the most experienced pilots would not have been capable of altering events, given that particular DC-10's structural defects and malfunctions.)

Perhaps one of the more futuristic applications of computer technology comes from the newly emerging discipline of biocybernetics, the linking of brain to machine. Already existing biocybernetic applications include computer-assisted devices that respond to commands as subtle as changes in a person's eye position: Twin brothers John and James Bertera of the OptoCom Research Group of Hadley, Massachusetts, recently developed a typing system that severely paralyzed or motor-impaired persons can learn to control with their eyes. By means of a comfortable eye-tracking system, the immobilized individual stares briefly at the letters on a computer-controlled key display.

The process is similar to ordinary typing except in the OptoCom system the measured position of the eye, or where the operator is looking, is substituted for finger and hand movements. The intention to type a particular letter is encoded by the duration of eye fixation. After several hours of practice with the system, volunteers achieved a speed of 18 words per minute of original composition with few errors.

Another biocybernetic advance soon to be available is an automated computer-assisted pen that captures the "dynamics" of individual signatures. Designed by Dr. Hewitt D. Crane of SRI International (formerly the Stanford Research Institute) in Menlo Park, California, the pen measures stress forces in three dimensions which are then converted to electrical signals and stored in the computer. Thus an imposter could not forge a signature by tracing, since, dynamically, the stress patterns in the hands and fingers of someone signing his name could be as unique and identifying as fingerprints.

There are also indications that eye movements can be clues to a person's cognitive and emotional states. For instance, it has been found that a person's eyes tend quickly to latch onto a picture corresponding to a spoken word. Thus, by projecting on a screen an array of different objects, a French teacher could instantaneously test whether or not a student understood <u>chien</u> as dog. If he did, his eyes would immediately pass over cats and cows and pigs, and home in on the drawing of a dog.

Foreign language learning could be speeded up immeasurably this way, according to Dr. Roger Cooper, developer of the system and director of the Center for Eye Movement Applications in Palo Alto. The teacher would not have to ask Johnny whether he knows a word. Johnny's eye movements would automatically give him away.

In the meantime, biocybernetic projects are providing some exciting and potentially useful applications of AI. For instance, in 1980, the University of London's AI and Robotic Unit at Queen Mary College began a series of studies aimed at developing cooperative ventures between machine and human intelligence in manipulating hostile environments. Underwater exploration, planetary investigation and nuclear plant inspection and management will be among the possible applications. But before achieving more complex marvels of biocybernetic communication, scientists first will have to understand a great deal more about how the human brain actually works, gathers information, and communicates.

How does the brain extract meaning from a visual scene, for instance? Even simple acts of facial recognition which we all perform routinely involve subtleties of pattern recognition that perhaps no AI device will ever be capable of duplicating.

In addition to difficulties in pattern recognition there are other problems. For one thing, language involves emotional connotations beyond the comprehension of present AI devices. Nevertheless, there are indications that artificial intelligence may yet make contributions to matters of emotional importance.

Researchers at UCLA recently reported on a computer program called PARRY that simulates the linguistic behavior of paranoid patients. This AI effort, using the SUMEX computer at Stanford with terminals in Los Angeles and Irvine, promises to provide a new understanding of paranoid thinking, along with more effective ways of treating patients. Other programs have been designed to aid in treating autistic children who traditionally avoid human contact.

In one surprising experiment with this program, psychiatrists were free to ask any question except direct inquiries regarding the identity of a "patient." In half the cases the patients were really previously diagnosed paranoids who had volunteered for the experiment. The other 50 percent of the responses came from the "paranoid" computer program. The results: experienced psychiatrists were able to score no better than at chance level when it came to telling the patient from the computer.

A test to determine whether machines could think was first suggested in 1950 by the British logician and computer pioneer, Alan M. Turing. The former World War II decoding expert was intrigued with the then-revolutionary possibility of a thinking machine. Such a machine would be capable, he speculated, of fooling an interrogator into uncertainty as to whether or not the respondent to a question was a man or a machine. Now the results of the paranoid experiments leave little doubt that AI machines are capable of fooling even the most experienced psychiatrists, at least in the area of paranoia.

But artificial intelligence machines may still have ample cause for modesty. Humans discovered long ago that brains aren't everything, and computers recently learned a similar lesson during a maze-running contest designed for electronic mice. Under the aegis of the Institute of Electrical and Electronics Engineers, the Amazing Micro-Mouse Maze Contest was conceived as a challenge to engineers and computer scientists to design a self-contained maze-solving electronic mouse that could negotiate an unknown maze by use of its own logic and memory. More than 6,000 world-wide entrants registered for the contest, and trial runs were held from coast to coast, leading up to a final race at the National Computer Conference in New York in June 1980.

Engineers came up with an ingenious array of entries which banged, sniffed, and learned their way through mazes at the trials, using a variety of sensing devices (from spring-loaded whiskers to "eyes" that could peek over the walls) and battery-operated "brains," or microprocessors. Many of the mice encountered unexpected problems. One of the smarter mice, named Cattywampus, lacked adequate speed control: it simply roared down the opening straight-away, slammed into a wall and got stuck there, unable to negotiate a turn it knew it should make.

In early trials, one of the faster mice was Moonlight Special. It was equipped with optical sensors and a microcomputer that allowed it to negotiate the maze, learning from its own errors as it went, without ever touching the walls. It was built by six engineers from the Battelle Northwest Research Laboratories in Richland, Washington, out of parts that cost them only $300.

But Moonlight Special was outrun at its debut by a comparative moron, a mouse named Harvey Wallbanger. The creation of three engineers from Hewlett-Packard, Harvey sped through the maze, hugging the right wall at all times as it advanced. Although this was not the shortest route, it required no intelligence and allowed Harvey to make up in speed what it lacked in brains.

Alarmed by the prospect of losing the finals, the Batelle team entered not only a smarter, faster-learning version of their Moonlight Special, but also an optical wall hugger, the Moonlight Flash, with barely any brains at all. Where Harvey groped blindly, the Moonlight Flash had eyes which gave it a slight edge. When the finals were over, the Battelle team had won, but artificial intelligence had taken something of a beating. It was their dumb mouse that came in first.

12 VLSI: Implications for Science and Technology

John S. Mayo

Readers of the New York Herald Tribune's inside pages might have been enticed by a single-column headline on page 16 of the July 1, 1948, edition: "'Cat Whiskers' Replace Tubes to Run Radio." The accompanying article noted that Bell Telephone Laboratories had demonstrated a new device called the transistor, of which the reporter said: "The device is still in the laboratory stage, but engineers believe it will cause a minor revolution in the electronics industry."

In fact, the electronics revolution triggered by the invention of the transistor some 30 years ago is revolutionizing the world. It promises to be wider in impact and greater in scope than was the Industrial Revolution. The industrial revolution harnessed mechanical energy to augment the muscles. The electronics revolution is harnessing the electron to augment the mind of man. In a little over 30 years this extraordinary discovery has touched every part of the world and has exerted dramatic impact on the U.S. and its role in world society.

The driving force behind this modern revolution is the technologies that permit ever greater increases in the scale of circuit integration on monolithic silicon crystals. The outstanding feature of these technologies is that complex circuits can be built far more cheaply and reliably by putting them on a single chip of silicon. This is largely because thousands of minute circuit elements can be batch-produced on a chip along with the interconnecting wiring required to make up a circuit. An interconnecting "wire" on a silicon chip costs about one hundredth as much as a "wire" on a printed circuit board.

Every year since the integrated circuit industry began in 1960 the number of components per chip of silicon has about doubled over that of the previous year. We are now in the era of very large scale integrated (VLSI) circuits. Today over 150,000 components can be fabricated and interconnected on a single chip of silicon about one tenth the size of a postage stamp. The number of components per chip can be expected to grow dramatically for at least another 10 to 15 years. The remarkable progress already made through the electronics revolution to date will likely be dwarfed by tomorrow's accomplishments.

This revolution was born in basic research. It is a shining example of how a few brilliant minds, through exceeding diligence and dedication, can open up new fields in science and technology, pave the way for follow-up inventions, and influence society for generations to come. And the synergistic effect is profound: solid state electronics has made enormous contributions to allied fields such as computer science and telecommunications, and to others as diverse as entertainment, medicine, and space exploration.

Even the development of VLSI circuits themselves depends strongly on computers and test instruments made practical by application of innovations in solid state electronics. A primary example is computer aided design (CAD). In the last five years, complexity of metal-oxide-semiconductor chips has grown by almost two orders of magnitude, but thanks to CAD there has been no real increase in man-hours needed to design them. In fact, without the advanced analysis and extensive simulation techniques available through CAD, it would be totally impractical to design VLSI chips. With CAD it is altogether routine to turn around design of custom chips in weeks, instead of months or even years. If that seems like pulling oneself up by one's own bootstraps, that is precisely the picture: the integrated circuit industry today relies heavily on systems built with the industry's most advanced products.

VLSI offers five fundamental attributes. First and foremost is low-cost electronics. A high-quality digital logic gate, the basic building block of all digital systems, cost a few dollars 25 years ago. Today a quality logic gate costs a few tenths of a cent – a thousandfold reduction.

Second, VLSI offers remarkable reliability. A logic gate on today's VLSI chip has a mean time to failure almost a hundred thousand times greater than the logic gate of 25 years ago.

Third, VLSI offers small size. This is directly related to low cost. And in some applications, ranging from pocket calculators to spacecraft guidance systems, it is important for its own sake. The small-size factor also permits other space savings. For example, the digital memory for the first telephone electronic switching system (ESS) used magnetic devices and required a lineup of equipment frames 104 feet along the floor. With 16-kilobit VLSI memory chips in use today, the same amount of ESS memory occupies a fraction of one equipment frame; the size is being further reduced by a design in production in the early 1980s that uses 64-kilobit chips.

Fourth, VLSI can save energy. As more and more circuit elements are packed onto a silicon chip, the power per element is lowered. Parasitic circuit elements have a large influence on overall circuit power levels, and parasitic elements diminish in size as physical size goes down. Low power is important for portability. But even in very large data processing and telecommunications centers, cumulative power reductions in VLSI can be significant in controlling overall energy consumption.

Fifth, VLSI is a technology of the microscopic world. It has stimulated a wide range of developments for dealing with physical features of micron dimensions. VLSI lithographic tools, analytical tools, and instrumentation all stimulate and support allied industries. X-ray analysis machines and electron microscopes are commonplace in the VLSI industry and are increasingly applicable to other sciences and industries that deal with microscopic entities.

The outlook for the future is continued rapid progress in all five basic attributes. This progress carries especially important implications for basic science and technology, computer science, data processing, and communications.

BASIC SCIENCE AND TECHNOLOGY

Integrated circuit technology is making increasingly low-cost computation available; this is having a major impact on the basic sciences. Computers have vastly expanded the usable level of idea complexity across all areas of research, making tractable what previously would have been intractable, and thus augmenting and expediting the processes through which ideas must be validated. In turn, ideas about computers and their uses are by-products of research, development, and applications work in every field. These ideas stimulate the advancement of computer science and engineering.

During 1979 a large amount of computing was utilized to help uncover fundamental knowledge about the history of the early universe. Specifically, digital computation was used to automatically detect and classify faint objects in the sky. Enormous amounts of data were collected through a terrestrial telescope, then digitized and fed into computers that processed the data to enhance and analyze the images. VLSI is making such major computation resources available to increasingly large numbers of researchers. The results are sure to profoundly enhance the quest for new knowledge.

VLSI is also putting new types of devices into the hands of researchers. For example, a VLSI imaging device was used in carrying out the work on faint objects in the sky. Called a charged-coupled device (CCD), this device is a large VLSI chip. It contains arrays of light-sensitive elements of high quantum efficiency and is organized in a way that simplifies digital analysis. CCD imaging devices make possible powerful and superior television cameras and other image-sensing systems often needed in basic research.

VLSI, especially in the form of microcomputers, also adds new dimensions to test equipment. Precision control, error-free data recording, and real-time data manipulation and display are just a few of the powerful enhancements available as a result of advances in solid state electronics. VLSI is especially well matched to digital circuits, which are relatively simple to design and manufacture, offer broad performance tolerances, deal with robust signals, and are available at low cost. The use of digital techniques in measurement and instrumentation avoids the tyranny of linear analog relationships between input and output signals, and removes the drudgery of obtaining and processing large amounts of data. Digital systems make possible multiple, nonlinear relationships, yielding measurement instruments that are highly stable, sensitive, and versatile. Integrated instrumentation systems are evolving in which many types of diagnostic techniques can be accommodated simultaneously under computer control. These instrumentation and control frontiers will be extended dramatically in the future.

VLSI also promises to change the very old as well as the very new. It has no respect for time. For example, for centuries it has been most economical to store many types of information on paper. But the day is rapidly approaching when, in many applications, paper will be an expensive alternative to storage on silicon chips or on garnet substrates using magnetic bubbles. Reading printed text for other than pleasure may become an inefficient alternative to electronic information access. The technology of information recording and retrieval − perhaps last revolutionized by the invention of the printing press and largely unchanged until recently − will be shaken by VLSI. If the old approach based on ink and paper survives at all, it will likely be in the pleasure sector; the business sector will increasingly find solid state memories and associated computing resources much more attractive.

VLSI will also profoundly influence science education. Solid state electronics already has led to dramatic changes in the content of technical courses. This has been especially profound in the field of electrical engineering, where, over the past quarter century, the closely allied and fast-growing field of computer science has emerged. Within electrical engineering itself, a survey of several schools shows about half the junior year courses and most of the senior year courses are new or substantially changed as a result of engineering concepts impacted by the solid state revolution. A large part of this change reflects the growth of digital technology. Digital techniques are especially well matched to VLSI and are rapidly displacing analog techniques. Hence, a wide range of courses for design and use of digital systems has emerged. It is likely that the swift evolution in the content of engineering and computer science courses will continue as VLSI further extends the domain and capability of digital technology. VLSI also will influence education in general by bringing computer-paced instruction and personalized terminals for learning within the financial grasp of a large portion of the population. As a result, graded classrooms and group-oriented instruction may become as obsolete as the little red schoolhouse.

The implications of VLSI for basic science and technology are strongly coupled with the fundamental symbiosis between solid state technology and science. Basic science contributes to the technology of fabricating new microstructures; in turn this stimulates the quest for new science. As the VLSI revolution spreads, this relationship will greatly expand the frontiers of knowledge.

For example, as smaller and smaller circuit dimensions are sought, there will be much exploration of the ultimate limit to how much complexity can be incorporated in a chip of silicon. This is an ongoing endeavor in which the solid state industry has moved from an era when discrete devices a square millimeter in size were standard, to today's VLSI chips that include 5,000 or more devices per square millimeter. Some discrete high-frequency devices have been built with submicron dimensions, and there are indications that dimensions in the tens of nanometers are technologically feasible. Such dimensions are 100 times smaller (10,000 more elements in the same area) than the current state of the art and should lead to more than one billion components per chip.

How will we get there? Many answers will be provided by basic science.   In lithography, projection optic systems are capable of yielding minimum line widths of about one micron. Lithographic techniques based on electron beams, ion beams, and X-rays are being explored for even smaller dimensions. Each approach has both advantages and problems. For example, electron beam scanning offers great resolution and depth of field, but is limited by electron scattering effects in the resist and by backscattering from the substrate. Advanced chemistry promises to provide high resolution resists, while advances in materials science, combined with chemistry, will allow so-called "nanostructures" to be fabricated on films over substrates. In the process new knowledge, ranging from reaction kinetics to microfabrication techniques, is generated.

Another major field of discovery in the quest for smaller diameters is anisotropic etching. This is a rich field for discovery. The underlying science is still fragmentary, and observed results tend to be unpredictable. Nonetheless, there are indications that plasma physics will provide some of the new knowledge needed to keep etching technology in step with advances in lithography.

Once the fundamental technological limits of VLSI and the practical factors that control those ultimate limits are known, an enormous amount of fundamental science will have been learned; it will have profound implications. The practical limits of low-voltage and low-current circuits and the interaction with noise sources, especially in digital devices, will be a revelation to electronics engineers. Investigations of lithographic techniques will spin off new capabilities in generation and control of light, X-rays, and electron beams, and their interaction with matter.

The extension of human capability in dealing with microscopic features to create miniscule patterns and to control chemical processes on such minute entities will have widespread implications. There are already signs that the limits will not stop short of structuring matter itself — building new materials and new structures a few atoms at a time. Already superlattices fabricated through molecular beam epitaxy have yielded structures with unusually high electron mobilities. Considering the powerful science that has been built upon nature's natural elements, there must be enormous potential impact in expanding available matter to include materials built a few atoms at a time from combinations of the atoms in the natural elements.

COMPUTER SCIENCE AND DATA PROCESSING

The revolutionary impact of VLSI on computer science and data processing stems directly from low cost. The first cost of large computing machines to process data decreased by a factor of about 1,000 between 1960 and 1980. Use of mid-sized machines or minicomputers can often reduce cost by another factor of five. Microcomputers on single chips of silicon are well matched to many jobs, reducing costs for these jobs by another factor of 100. Microcomputers are available today for just a few dollars each. They can do many of the computing jobs that just 20 years ago required machines costing several hundred thousand dollars.

When those high-cost machines were the only computers available, the jobs had to be brought to the computer. Large computation centers had to be kept fully loaded to be economical, and computer scientists usually were found — in limited numbers — in the vicinity of those large computers. With computing so much less expensive today, jobs less often have to be collected and brought to the computation center; the computer increasingly is being brought to the job. And every computer does not have to be used all the time to make it economical. The computer, like a hand drill, may spend much of its time idle, waiting to be used. Also like a hand drill, the computer can be sized to fit a particular job. Large numbers of computer scientists now work in the vicinity of the job, hand-in-hand with the engineers. In many cases the computer scientist has become the person in charge.

By making low-cost computing resources widely available, the electronics revolution has generated an insatiable appetite for computer programmers and software architects. There simply is not enough talent to program all the computers that can now be economically deployed. A microcomputer may cost only a few dollars and be manufactured by the millions. A program for that microcomputer may cost tens or even hundreds of thousands of dollars.

To put it bluntly, computer science has not yet provided enough science and the productivity improvement tools that are required to fully utilize VLSI technology. Much of the answer may be found in VLSI itself. It is becoming increasingly possible to put portions of the software right on the chip. As a result, software people — programmers, systems analysts, even users — are actively involved with hardware people in designing microcomputers.

VLSI may do much more. It makes possible systems architectures that are more complex in hardware and simpler in software. These complex hardware architectures are opening a new field of software science — distributed software systems. Increasingly, large systems are controlled not by just one computer, but by a whole family of computers of many sizes. All are orchestrated via centralized software control. Computer science is only now beginning to yield knowledge applicable in designing such systems. VLSI, by increasing the demands on computer science, is stimulating the generation and flow of knowledge needed to make the design of distributed software systems into a science. It will be a long time coming, however: even discrete software design remains more of an art than a science.

COMMUNICATIONS

Data processing and telecommunications are both extensions of the mind. They speed up mental processes by greatly reducing the time required for doing analysis and for interacting with other minds and machines. It is no wonder that the impact of VLSI on telecommunications is nearly as profound as it is on data processing. As each new milestone in scale of integration reduces circuit costs per function, a wider range of sophisticated telecommunications equipment becomes economically feasible.

The evolution of the nationwide telecommunications network is largely driven by the ever-expanding use of stored program control, itself made practical by the solid state revolution. In stored program control, a system such as a telephone switcher is built to include a digital processor that can be programmed to control the system. Service features can be changed readily by modifying the control program. The telecommunications network now contains thousands of these stored program-controlled systems: it is the largest distributed processing network in the world.

The implications of this network are immense. Already a business customer can enjoy private network services and a great degree of control over his own service features. VLSI also makes it practical for private branch exchanges (PBXs) to provide stored program control directly on a customer's premises, and to offer some of the stored program power of such electronic PBXs in key telephone systems for smaller businesses.

Nor is the power of stored program control in telecommunications confined to private network services. Largely through software changes, the network's processors will be programmed to provide a host of new, innovative voice services to the public. Candidate services range from screening of incoming calls to voting by telephone, nationwide emergency 911 service, improved INWATS services, personal nationwide telephone numbers, and many more. VLSI-based repertory dialer telephones, which permit one-button dialing of frequently called numbers, already are available to both business and residential customers, and smarter, all-electronic telephones are imminent.

Many advanced public telecommunications capabilities are either available or are being demonstrated now. Electronic switchers provide such custom calling services as call forwarding, abbreviated dialing, call waiting notification, and add-on conference calling. Additional call forwarding and call storage features are being tested. Advanced Mobile Telephone Service, which can offer quality telephone service to large numbers of people in vehicles, is working well on a trial basis in Chicago. And the British have a system called VIEWDATA that couples the home television set via telephone equipment to various libraries and other information services. It enables one to call up data from memory banks stocked by private suppliers of news, home entertainment, and business services, and display them on the home receiver.

VLSI will make possible a concept that has been largely a fantasy until now – machines that speak, listen, and act upon command. Machines that generate speech, such as those that report changed telephone numbers, have been in use for some time. But a machine that can recognize your voice, call you by name, and respond to your spoken command is a more difficult thing. It is a long sought-after communication interface between human and machine, offering great potential in communications, education, transaction, and reservation systems, as well as a vast array of other information services.

Such machines exist today – especially in research laboratories. Their widespread use depends on cost reductions, because voice recognition and synthesis systems require highly complex electronics to achieve useful vocabularies and swift response. Advances in VLSI helped provide the impetus for extensive research and development in this field, and VLSI will be the vehicle for the needed cost reductions. Small foreign language translators now being marketed are. based on VLSI memory and logic chips; they represent just the tip of the thrust of VLSI into other aspects of communications. With further advances in VLSI, as well as in computer science and behavioral research, people will increasingly communicate with their machines by talking to them. Increasingly, the machines will respond by talking back.

The falling cost of digital circuits is creating other opportunities in communications. When digital circuits cost a dollar a gate, they had to be used sparingly. Now that logic gates cost only a few tenths of a cent each, they can be applied economically almost everywhere. For example, echoes on telephone circuits carried via satellites have been a problem. A way to cancel out these echoes was invented some time ago. But the digital devices needed to implement echo cancellation were too expensive to be deployed on each telephone circuit. Until recently each echo canceler required a cabinet full of equipment about the size of a home refrigerator at each end of each telephone circuit. This year Bell Laboratories put that entire circuit onto a single chip of silicon. Instantly it became quite practical to deploy echo cancelers, now in chip form, not only on satellite circuits but on long terrestrial circuits as well.

The echo canceler is but one example of the growing sophistication and economy of digital circuitry in telecommunications. Telephone service is increasingly being provided by digital facilities despite the fact that the human eardrum and larynx are analog instruments. These digital facilities can support a host of non-voice services such as high speed data, facsimile, graphics, and video. Such services are important components of the Information Age.

Microcomputers also are having a large impact on telecommunications. They are used extensively in processing signals, controlling and monitoring equipment, reporting failures, and in customizing communications interfaces for users' needs. They are especially effective in smart terminals that interface users with the telephone network. These smart terminals are at work today and, with increasing VLSI capability, they offer a potential that ranges from monitoring security from intrusion in the home to becoming a virtual secretary in the office.

CONCLUSION

The implications of VLSI on the basic sciences, on data processing, and on telecommunications flow into other fields too numerous to treat in detail. Low-cost data processing and expanded communications are of immeasurable value to almost every serious undertaking. Medicine is being changed by the VLSI-based technology that backs up the doctor with increasing amounts of computer support, and a vast array of complex, smart, and rapid test and diagnostic instruments. Further space exploration and use will depend on VLSI-based control and communications equipment. Energy development and conservation will benefit from smart, economical instruments and controls. Automotive operations such as carburetion, timing, etc., will increasingly operate under microprocessor control to improve fuel economy and reduce emissions. More and more chemical processes will be monitored and controlled by microcomputers to maintain product quality, reduce waste, and minimize air and water pollution.

VLSI is a powerful technology with profound implications for the future. It is a rich source of ideas and tools for a wide range of industries. Ultimately, it is up to society as a whole to determine how it uses the ideas and tools supplied by technology, and this holds true for VLSI. Society has eagerly accepted VLSI capabilities to date – ranging from high quality telecommunications and computing resources, to pocket calculators and digital wristwatches. This gives strong grounds for optimism that the ultimate potential of VLSI and the resulting implications for science and technology will be fully and swiftly realized.

Index

PRESTEL, 73
Printing and reproduction,
  66-8
Printing technology, 5-6
Productivity, office, 93,
  109
PSI Energy, 91

Rain, effect on satellite
  systems, 37-9
RC (remote concentrators),
  89
RCA (Radio Corporation of
  America), 10, 90
Regulation and communica-
  tion services, 72
RAM (Random Access Memory), 77
Robotic Unit, Queen Mary
  College, 129
ROM (Pre-Wired "read only
  memory"), 77

Sanyo, 18
Satellite Business Systems,
  65
Satellite circuits
  communications develop-
    ments and, 81-2
  outages and. 90
Satellite communication
  links, 35
Satellite signals and
  rain, 37-9
Satellite system, Canada,
  120
Satellite systems
  costs of, 22-4
  domestic and inter-
    national, 24-5
Satellites
  Canada, 120, 121
  Clarke, Arthur C., 34, 35
  domestic, 36-7
  fiber optics and, 122
  futuristic, 39-40
  Hermes, 120
  INTELSAT, 23, 24, 34-5
  Pierce, John and, 34
Scanners and information
  storage, 59-64

Schank, Roger L., 125
Science, basic, and VSLI,
  133
Secretaries and office
  work, 105-6
SECS, 125
Shared logic system, 96
Signature-recognition
  and computers, 127
SNETCO, xi
Software and information
  storage, 64, 81
Solid state devices, 3
Sony, 9, 18
Sound and digital
  technology, 12
Speech-recognition and
  computers, 124
SRI International, 127
Stamford Medical School, 125
Stereophonic sound, 7
Storage of information,
  59-64
  achival, 62, 64
  bubble technology, 61,
    62, 63, 84, 94
  discs, 61, 64
  optical discs, 62
  scanners, 59, 60
  software, 64
Storage technology and
  digital technology,
  11-2
Submarine cable and outages,
  24, 25, 26, 90
SUMEX, biomedical resource
  computer, 125
Sun transit and satellites,
  36, 38
Symbols as information,
  5-6

TASI (Time-Assigned Speech
  Interpolation), 26
TAT (Transatlantic Tele-
  phone Cable), 25
Tariffs and data
  transmission, 28
Taylor, Frederick W., 55

About the Editors and Contributors

THOMAS J.M. BURKE, co-editor of Communication Technologies and Information Flow, was Dean, Graduate School of Corporate and Political Communication, Fairfield University, in Fairfield, Connecticut. He founded the Center for the Advancement of Human Communication and wrote a television series, "Face of the World," for Westinghouse Broadcasting, dealing with forces affecting individuals in developing countries. Earlier in his career he had worked for Carl Byoir and Associates, a New York-based public relations firm. Dr. Burke, a Jesuit priest, was former religious editor of "America," and author of Public Relations of Religious Institutions in a Pluralistic Society. He received his B.A. and M.A. degrees from Boston College and his Ph.D. from the Graduate School of Public Administration, New York University. Deeply interested in the impact of electronics on communication, he organized seminars to delve into the frontiers of the new communication sciences. Dr. Burke passed away during the editing of this book.

MAXWELL LEHMAN, professor of political/governmental communication at Fairfield University, was formerly City Administrator of New York. He has been a senior public administration specialist for the Ford Foundation; vice-chairman for jurisdiction and structure, State Study Commission for New York City, and one of the authors of the present New York City charter. Professor Lehman lectures extensively around the world on problems of cities, and has written widely on urban affairs and government management. His academic experience has included teaching at the Graduate School of Public Administration, New York University, the Ecole Nationale d'Administration in Tunis, and Long Island University. His education was at Rutgers University, Harvard University, and New York University. He holds the title of scholar-in-residence at the Urban Academy for Management in New York.

JOSEPH AGRESTA, a member of Union Carbide's internal consulting group, has participated in the development of Union Carbide's long-range plan for the introduction of office technology and provided consulting services for early installations of word processing and associated technologies. His other interests include the development of financial planning models and strategic planning systems. Previously he was a research scientist, primarily in the area of applied nuclear science, for Union Carbide, United Nuclear Corporation, and Curtiss-Wright Corporation. Dr. Agresta received his Bachelor of Electrical Engineering degree from Cooper Union, his Master of Science and Doctor of Philosophy degrees from New York University.

B.H. BURDINE is a Research Manager at General Telephone and Electronics Laboratories in Waltham, Massachusetts, where he is responsible for developments in digital telephones, fiber-optic transmission, and satellite systems. Prior to joining GTE in 1965, he was on the teaching staff at Mississippi State University and did research on antennas at the Massachusetts Institute of Technology, where he earned the masters degree. His current activities include several K-band satellite propagation experiments, development of improved antennas for satellite earth stations, and design of fiber-optic links for digital telephones and CATV systems.

E. BRYAN CARNE, Director of Communications Products Technology Center, General Telephone and Electronics Laboratories, Inc., is responsible for research and development work in advanced telecommunications including: earth stations, optical fiber transmission systems, optical components and devices, digital subscriber equipment, mixed service local systems, software engineering, computer-aided design, custom LSI circuit design, etc. Dr. Carne received his Bachelor of Science degree in Engineering and his Ph.D. from the University of London. He has done post-graduate work in advanced management at Harvard. He has published extensively, including a book on artificial intelligence techniques.

LEE L. DAVENPORT is a consultant in telecommunication planning and advanced technology. He retired early in 1981 from General Telephone and Electronics Corporation, where he had served as Vice President-Chief Scientist at corporate headquarters in Stamford, Conn. Prior to that, he had been for 15 years President of GTE Laboratories. Dr. Davenport has specialized in interpreting the impact of new technology and forecasting future trends in the telecommunications and information fields. He was also spokesman before governmental, public and private organizations with respect to technical areas. Dr. Davenport joined GTE Sylvania in 1957, a GTE subsidiary, and became President of the Sylvania-Corning Nuclear Corporation.

LYNN W. ELLIS is Vice-President for Engineering, Bristol-Babcock Instruments & Systems, in Waterbury, Connecticut. He was formerly director of research, International Telephone and Telegraph Corporation, supervising worldwide activities in applied research and advanced technology, and served as executive director of the ITT Research Council. Previously he was responsible for groups in that company's Headquarters Technical Department controlling worldwide development and engineering in wire and radio transmission, digital systems, telecommunications planning, and engineering standardization. His experience with ITT embraced technical work in the operating and manufacturing sectors of telecommunications, as well as research and development in military electronics. Dr. Ellis spent 11 years overseas in engineering management positions in ITT subsidiaries. He became assistant managing director of ITT's principal Australia telecommunications manufacturing company, STC (Pty) Ltd. He is a Fellow of the Institute of Electrical and Electronic Engineers and of the American Association for the Advancement of Science. He was Chairman of the Telecommunications Equipment Advisory Committee to the U.S. Department of Commerce from 1973 to 1975. He earned his Bachelor of Electrical Engineering degree from Cornell University, his Master of Science degree from Stevens Institute of Technology, and his Doctor of Professional Studies in Management degree from Pace University.

RICHARD J. HAYES is Director of Technology Investment Planning at Xerox Corporation in Stamford, Connecticut. He is responsible for the development of an overall technology investment strategy. His previous Xerox positions include Vice President, Copier Product Engineering and Vice President, Advanced Business Planning. He holds B.S., M.S., M.B.A., and Ph.D. degrees.

J.R. MARCHAND is Secretary of the Interdepartmental Committee on Space, Department of Communications, Ottawa, Canada. Previously, as Director of the Rural Communications Program, he was concerned with improving rural communications, both narrow and broad-band, in Canada through the use of new technologies (satellites, fiber optics, carrier concentrators, digital techniques), and assessing social, economic, and financial implications. He has held numerous positions in the governmental-scientific area, as Science Councellor to the Canadian Embassy in Paris, as Executive Secretary of The Interim Communications Satellite Committee of INTELSAT, and as Director General, International Communications, Department of Communication. He has been a member of the Canadian delegation to a session of the United Nations working group on satellite broadcasting and has served with various other delegations, in many parts of the world. Mr. Marchand's formal education was at the University of Manitoba. In addition, he has studied Modern Network Synthesis at the University of Ottawa, and has taken course work in various other educational institutions, in management techniques and computer programming. He is a member of the International Institute of Communications and of the Canadian Science and Technical Society.

RAYMOND W. MARSHALL is Vice President and General Manager, Systems Operations Department, General Electric Information Services Company. A graduate of Case Institute of Technology (B.S.E.E.) and Syracuse University (M.B.A.), Mr. Marshall joined the Heavy Military Electronics Department in 1957, following service in the U.S. Navy. He has been Program Manager on radar, sonar, computer, and data systems projects; Manager, Computer Systems Engineering in Special Information Products Department; Program Manager, Advanced Time Sharing Systems; Manager, Network Systems; General Manager, Information Services Systems Department; General Manager, Information Services Systems and Technology Department; and General Manager, Information Services Systems Operations Department.

JOHN S. MAYO is Executive Vice President, Network Systems, and was formerly Vice President for Electronics Technology at Bell Laboratories in Murray Hill, New Jersey. Initially concerned with research on transistorized digital computers and use of digital computers in defense systems, he turned to the development of transmission systems utilizing pulse code modulation techniques. He was responsible for the development of the T1 carrier repeater, several high-speed PCM projects, and the D2 channel bank. He also worked on the command decoder and switching unit for the TELSTAR communications satellite project and was involved in the development of methods for transmitting PICTUREPHONE® signals. In 1967, he became director of the Ocean Systems Development Laboratory, with responsibility for the development of electronic systems for use in the ocean. He became executive director of the Ocean Systems Division, and then executive director of the Toll Electronic Switching Division. In 1975 Dr. Mayo became responsible for directing design and development of efficient, low-cost, high-reliability electronics components and associated technologies for use in the telephone companies, and for directing design and development activities to provide energy sources, power supplies, and building environment designs for the Operating Telephone Companies. He assumed his present assignment in 1979, and is responsible for Research and Development Systems for the Telephone Network and the electronics technology those systems use. Dr. Mayo received his B.S., M.S., and Ph.D. degrees in electrical engineering from North Carolina State University. He was co-recipient of the Alexander Graham Bell Medal in 1978.

P.E. PASHLER is currently Vice President, Corporate Technology, Canadian General Electric Company Ltd. Formerly Manager of Electronics Technology Evaluation at General Electric's Corporate Research and Development Center in Schenectady, New York, he headed a group of senior scientists and engineers charged with the assessment of new electronic and information technologies. In a previous position, Dr. Pashler managed the Signal Electronics Laboratory of GE's Corporate Research Center, where he supervised the research and development activities of over a hundred scientists engaged in activities ranging from the exploration of physical phenomena to the invention of new electronic devices and the development of advanced electronic systems. Major contributions include GE's Talaria large-screen television projector, a variety of imaging devices, surface charge transistor technology, digital memories, and computerized tomography. Earlier, as an individual researcher, he built some of the first experimental X-ray image intensifiers for medical purposes. He also contributed to developments in television camera tubes, electron optics, and the technology of photosensitive surfaces. During World War II, Dr. Pashler was engaged in military developments for the National Research Council of Canada. Following the war, Dr. Pashler was on the staff of the Physics Department at the University of Toronto. He held a Post-Doctoral Fellowship at the VanderWalls Laboratory of the University of Amsterdam, Holland, in molecular physics.

RICHARD M. RESTAK is a physician who heads the Restak Neurological Associates in Washington, D.C. As is clear from his contribution, which originally appeared in Smithsonian, he is a man of broad general interests beyond his own specialized field of neurological medicine. Dr. Restak is on the faculty of Georgetown University and the Washington School of Psychiatry. He is the author of Premeditated Man and of The Brain: The Last Frontier, a section of which deals with the man-machine inter-relationship. His medical degree is from Georgetown University.

JAMES M. WEST is corporate manager of office systems support for Xerox. Since joining Xerox in 1964, he has held key administrative management positions in the field sales organizations in New York and the Greenwich area. Most recently he was branch administrative operations manager within the Northeast Region Headquarters. Before that, he held various headquarters assignments in customer relations and field marketing support. He holds a bachelor's degree in business administration from Oregon State University.